THE JOY OF SLIMMING

Margaret Allan is the pseudonym of a scientist
who has made a special study of excess weight
and its problems. She is a member of the
scientific staff at the Clinical Research Centre
of the Medical Research Council and has
previously been employed by the Consumers'
Association as Research Officer for their
Which? Slimming Guide.

Married and aged 27, Margaret Allan experienced
fatness in her teens – and she has
successfully stayed slim ever since.

The Joy of Slimming

Margaret Allan

CORONET BOOKS
Hodder and Stoughton

Printed and bound in Great Britain
for Coronet Books.
Hodder and Stoughton, London,
by Hazell Watson & Viney Ltd,
Aylesbury, Bucks

ISBN 0 340 20652 7

Contents

To my husband – for his gallant slimming effort

Acknowledgements

During the writing of this book I have had much help and encouragement from my family, my friends and my professional colleagues. I should like to thank them all, particularly Dr. John Atha for his help with writing Chapter 11, Exercise and Slimming.

I am also grateful to the Consumers' Association and to Slimming Magazine Ltd for allowing me to mention the results of their tests.

Introduction

THIS IS not the first book to be written for slimmers by any means – nor is it likely to be the last. My aim throughout the book is to show you how slimming can be simplified. The way to get slim can be summed up quite simply in the following paragraph:

The human body needs a certain amount of energy to run on – just as a car needs fuel. You supply the body with this fuel in the form of food and drink. Once your body has sufficient fuel, it will convert the surplus food and drink into a storage reserve – this is FAT. The only time that your body needs to use its reserve fuel store is when the fuel supply from food and drink is not adequate. So, cutting down the energy value of the food and drink you consume is the only way of getting rid of fat.

The theory is simple, putting it into practice is far from easy:

First, you have got to convince yourself of the advantages of being slim and the disadvantages of being fat. This will give you the incentive you need to start and the determination you need to succeed.

Secondly, you should know enough about the basic principles of nutrition and physiology to distinguish the sensible advice from the many false promises and red herrings that you are likely to come across. This way you will not be disappointed.

Thirdly, you have got to make sure that you choose the method that is best for you as an individual – no two people get fat for the same reason, and no two people will achieve equal success with the same slimming method.

Lastly, you have got to stick to your method until you are slim and then find a sensible way of adapting it so that you *stay* that way.

The fact that you are reading this book at all probably means that you are thinking about slimming. The first chapter will help you decide whether you really need to slim and convince you that, if you do, you will find it worthwhile.

Once you have decided that you are going to slim, you will find all the information you need in the first few chapters. There is a short section explaining the basic principles of nutrition and how your body deals with the different foods you eat. Then the two basic methods of eating less – calorie cutting and carbohydrate cutting – are described. The advantages and disadvantages of each are discussed and you should be able to choose the one which is most likely to work for you.

After you have decided which type of dieting method you should follow, the following chapters will help you put it into practice:

● *If you like to plan all your meals from scratch – you will find the fully comprehensive food value list indispensable when you want to work out how many calories or how much carbohydrate there is in a certain food.*

7

- *If you are preparing the food yourself, you will find lots of helpful tips in the general section about cooking to help you produce interesting meals using methods that will not fatten you too much.*
- *If you like to follow specific recipes when you are slimming, you will find that the basic recipe section is arranged so that you can cook dishes and know just how fattening they are. What I have tried to do in this section is to give you a wide selection of basic recipes for each type of food, e.g. meat, eggs, cheese, desserts, sauces etc. The number of calories and the amount of carbohydrate is given for a one person portion of each dish. The recipes are indexed clearly in two ways. So if you fancy an egg dish you can easily pick one with a suitable number of calories to fit in with the rest of your day's eating. Or, if you want some ideas for poultry dishes with no carbohydrate you can look down the list and see what appeals to you.*
- *If your mind goes completely blank when you start adding up figures and you would rather have a definite menu plan to follow when you are slimming, this book is for you as well. There is a section which suggests meals which you can eat during the day. Calorie cutters will find a selection of daily menus which will limit them to approximately 1,000 Calories. Carbohydrate cutters will find plenty of suggested menus for keeping their day's intake of carbohydrate below 50 grammes. Whichever method you choose, you will find enough 'day plans' suggested to let you have plenty of variety in what you eat without having to do any counting yourself.*

Some of you, of course, might be reading this book not because you yourself are fat but because you think that someone else in your family could be a bit slimmer. This is the reason for the chapter on 'Slimming the family'. If your husband or children are not keen to slim, you will find hints on how to cook meals for them which are not too fattening and which should help to slim them without their being aware of eating anything drastically different. In this section too, is some advice for mothers on how to feed their babies and young children.

The next part of the book is all about exercise and its place in slimming. If you are the type of person who considers chess an energetic game, you need not read this chapter. But if you would like some advice about the best exercise to take when you are slimming, you should find it here.

If you read the main body of the book, you will know everything you really need to know about getting slim. But the trouble with slimming is that it is one of those subjects surrounded by old wives' tales which confuse you, and false claims that mislead you. So, the last part of the book is in the form of a Slimmers' Forum, which answers some of the many questions that are often asked by would-be slimmers.

CHAPTER ONE

Should You Be Slimming?

IF YOU WANT to get slim it is probably for one or more of the following reasons:

- *You want to look more attractive*
- *You feel that society caters more for slim people, e.g. sizes of clothes*
- *You want to be healthier.*

Men are probably more likely to be motivated by the last factor and women by the first two.

Only *you* will know how fat you have to be before you feel unattractive or are driven to utter frustration in shops because the clothes you like no longer fit. The only good guidelines you have are a full length mirror and your own conscience. You will probably have a good idea when you notice that your waistband is getting tighter and you have to hold your breath in to do up your zip.

Sometimes other people can be helpful. Some will whisper in a friendly fashion that you should lose some weight; others will tell you less kindly. Their brutal remarks might give you just the determination you need to show them that you *can* get slim. If *you* think you are fat but everyone else says that they like you as you are, you will have to show even greater determination.

Society, of course, as well as fashion, dictates which shapes and weights are acceptable. An explorer in nineteenth-century Africa found one tribe where the men were so keen to fatten up their women that young girls were made to suck milk continually, and were beaten if they stopped sucking. They grew into women who were so fat that they had to grovel around like seals on the floors of the huts.

In fact, it has really only been in the last few decades that Western civilisation has stopped thinking of the fat person as a symbol of well-being and content-ment. The image of the 'jolly fat man' is a fast disappearing one.

During this time, evidence has been rapidly accumulating to show that fatness carries a serious health risk and that it really *is* better to be slim. The trouble is that it is very difficult to tell you exactly how slim you *should* be and the actual health risk caused by your fatness. Although doctors and scientists agree that being fat is bad for you, they are not in complete agreement about some aspects of the relevant data.

The figures usually quoted are those of the Metropolitan Life Insurance Company of America. They listed 'desirable' heights and weights which were established on the basis of weights associated with lowest mortality and related to frame size and age.

9

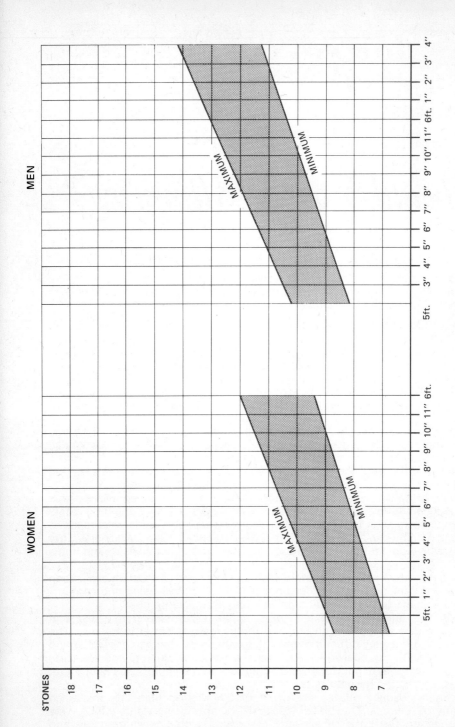

TABLE OF DESIRABLE WEIGHTS

Because it is difficult to decide which frame size you are (a purely arbitrary judgment at the best of times) the Life Insurance figures are shown in the form of a graph on page 10. This graph shows weight plotted on the vertical axis against height plotted on the horizontal axis. The MAXIMUM line joins together those points which indicate the maximum allowed weight for a large framed person of different heights. Similarly, the MINIMUM line shows the minimum weight expected for small framed people. To use this graph, draw an imaginary line between your height (without shoes) and your weight in indoor clothes. If the point at which they meet falls somewhere within the shaded area then you are not medically overweight. If it falls above the maximum line, you are. Of course if you are particularly small-framed (you take a particularly small size in shoes and gloves) you should not be satisfied unless your weight is in the lower half of the shaded area.

The Health Risk

The data collected by the life insurance company implied that if you are at least 20 per cent above your desirable weight your chances of dying earlier are greater than a person of the same age who is not overweight. The more overweight you are the greater the risk you face.

Being fat is also associated with a variety of complications and illnesses. Fat people move around less than people of normal weight, so it stands to reason that this slowness in movement will make them more likely to have accidents at home or at work.

The extra weight the joints and ligaments have to carry is probably responsible for the mechanical complications that often afflict fat people such as pain in the back and knees and shortness of breath.

Then there are metabolic complications associated with fatness – the most important associations are those between obesity and diabetes, and heart and kidney diseases.

So, all in all, and without wishing to dwell too long on these rather morbid thoughts, you really do have a much better chance of a healthy life if your weight is normal. Just think of it this way – if you were going to travel by a heavy aeroplane and someone told you that the heavy plane was much more likely to crash than a lighter one, which would you choose?

To end on a somewhat cheerier note, the same insurance company also looked at a group of people who had once been overweight but were now slim to see how they fared when it came to assessing their health risk. It was found that they had no extra risk at all – a very encouraging finding.

CHAPTER TWO

Food and Energy

AS I EXPLAINED in the Introduction, getting slim is all a matter of adjusting your energy balance, i.e. the ratio between the energy value of the food and drink you have and the energy you use up in living. Let us look at this energy in more detail.

First, we must introduce the unit used to measure energy value – the calorie. In physics, one calorie is the amount of heat needed to raise the temperature of 1 gramme of water one degree of temperature (measure on the Centigrade scale). Nutritionists use a unit which is 1,000 times larger so it is either written as Calorie or as kilo Calorie. The total energy value of any food or drink, measured in Calories, depends on the nutrients it contains.

Food

All too often, people who are overweight tend to 'live to eat' rather than 'eat to live'. The essential facts that you should know about food to help you slim sensibly are dealt with very briefly below.

Most foods contain a mixture of different nutrients, although some, e.g. sugar and butter, contain only one. The ideal diet is one which is sufficiently well balanced to supply your body with enough of these nutrients for its day to day needs, while at the same time being tasty and pleasant enough to satisfy you – so that you do not want to overeat. There are four different types of nutrients which you need:

> *Proteins* provide the basic material for growth and repair of body cells and tissues. They supply the building materials for hormones and enzymes – two important groups of regulating substances. Once they have done this primary job, your body can convert them into glucose for energy. If no more energy is needed, the glucose is turned into fat.
>
> *Fats* provide a concentrated energy source if needed. Otherwise they are stored in fat depots.
>
> *Carbohydrates* are only really important as energy sources. Too much carbohydrate can be converted into fat and stored.
>
> *Minerals and vitamins* are found associated with the other nutrients and although the body only needs comparatively small quantities of them they are very important because they regulate most body processes. The Table on page 13 indicates the best sources of food for the most important of them.

VITAMINS

Vitamins	Role	Best sources
A	Growth. Vision. Protection against infections.	Liver, butter, margarine, carrots, spinach, apricots, watercress, cheese and eggs.
B group	Growth. Protection against infections of the nervous system and skin.	Meat, liver, flour, bread, cereals, eggs, cheese, milk and leafy green vegetables.
C	Growth. Protection of tissues.	Potatoes, green vegetables and fresh citrus fruits.
D	Bone formation.	Fish, margarine, eggs, butter, liver (and sunlight).
E	Not yet definitely known in man.	Vegetable oils, wheat germ, margarine and eggs.
K	Blood clotting mechanism.	Dark green vegetables.

MINERALS

Mineral	Role	Best sources
Calcium	Bone and teeth formation. Blood clotting mechanism. Muscle functioning.	Milk, cheese, bread and green vegetables.
Iron	Blood functioning. Muscle functioning.	Offal, meat, eggs, cereal products and green vegetables.
Sodium	Maintaining composition of body and cell fluids.	Bacon, smoked fish, cheese and bread (and, of course, table salt)
Potassium	Maintaining composition of body and cell fluids.	Vegetables and meat.
Iodine	Thyroid functioning.	Fish and shellfish.

Although water has not been included as a nutrient, it is also essential for life. It transports food to the body cells and carries away the waste products. So you must have it for a well balanced diet.

Proteins, fats and carbohydrates can occur in both complex and simple forms. The reason you have a digestive system is to make sure that all the complex forms which are present in the food you eat are broken down into their corresponding simpler forms before they are absorbed into your blood stream and transported to the cells of your body. The long *protein* chains are broken down into their constituent *amino acids*. The large fat molecules are broken down into smaller fatty acids and the multi-unit carbohydrate molecules are broken down into single units. Once these basic units are inside your cells, together with the necessary vitamins and minerals, they can undergo a series of reactions to produce energy as the end result.

Energy

You will make use of this energy in many different forms. For example, some will be used to keep your body temperature constant, some as mechanical energy to make your muscles work, and some as electrical energy to send messages through your nervous system. However, when we want to talk about the energy value of food it is more convenient to imagine that all the energy is converted into heat. So when scientists want to know the precise calorie value of food they can ignite it (in oxygen at a very high pressure) and measure the heat given off. However, it is more usual to calculate the energy value of a food from an analysis of its protein, fat and carbohydrate content. Conversion factors have been worked out to give a reasonably accurate value for the amount of energy your body actually obtains from *pure* nutrients:

1 gramme carbohydrate supplies $3\frac{3}{4}$ Calories
1 gramme protein   supplies 4   Calories
1 gramme fat   supplies 9   Calories
1 gramme alcohol   supplies 7   Calories

Here is an example to show how nutritionists can work out the calorie values of food:

Knowing that an ounce of white bread contains 15·4 gm. carbohydrate, 0·5 gm. fat and 2·4 gm. protein, the energy value can be calculated at about 70 Calories per ounce:

$$15·5 \times 3·75 = 58·1 \text{ Calories from carbohydrate}$$
$$0·5 \times 9 \quad = \quad 4·5 \text{ Calories from fat}$$
$$2·4 \times 4 \quad = \quad 9·6 \text{ Calories from protein}$$

$$\overline{72 \quad \text{Calories}}$$

Because water contains no calories at all, it follows that watery foods contain fewer calories than drier foods, e.g. an ounce of potato contains 5·9 gm. carbohydrate and 0·6 gm. protein. So a raw potato which is about 80 per cent water has an energy value of about 25 Calories per ounce.

As has already been said, the purpose of eating fats and carbohydrates is to

14

supply you with energy and, although protein has other more important uses, it can also be used as energy. So you must think of all foods as supplying you with calories which are either used for energy or otherwise stored as fat.

A certain amount of energy is needed to perform all the involuntary bodily processes of life, e.g. to keep your heart beating, to keep breathing, to keep your body temperature at 98·4°F. etc. This all requires somewhere in the region of 1,000 to 2,000 Calories each day. You would need this amount of energy even if you stayed in bed, resting all day. On top of this 'resting metabolic energy', you need extra energy for all the voluntary movements you do, e.g. sitting, standing, walking, running, etc. Usually, the more these activities exhaust you, the more energy you are using to do them.

The sum of your 'resting metabolic energy' and your 'voluntary energy' will add up to the total amount of energy you use in a particular day. An average young adult male will use up something like 2,500 to 3,500 Calories a day while his wife will use up about 1,800 to 2,500 Calories. If you want to make a guess at what your own daily energy expenditure is, you should remember the following points :

1. Growing processes require extra energy. This is why the energy required by children, adolescents and pregnant women is relatively high.
2. Bigger people need more energy for certain tasks, just as cars with bigger engines need more petrol. (If you are very large now and have a lot of weight to lose, you must remember that you will not need so much energy when you have reduced your size.)
3. As you get older, your 'resting metabolic energy' tends to decrease, i.e. it costs less to run your body (quite the opposite from an old car which costs more to run because it usually needs more petrol the older it gets). Not only this, but your 'voluntary energy' will also tend to decrease as you become less active.

So, at last we have got back to our basic energy balance equation. You will stay a reasonably constant weight if :

$$\text{Total energy in} = \text{Total energy out}.$$

As soon as your body has a surplus amount of energy it will store it in some convenient form so that later on it can draw on this reserve if supplies get low. The most economic storage form your body has is fat. At 250 Calories per ounce, it really is a concentrated store. The fat is stored in fat cells which are grouped together as fat deposits in various places in your body. Compare this situation with that of finding you have enough money to save some. You need an efficient storage method and so instead of stuffing your piggy bank full of small coins you hand the money into your bank who will store it in a more convenient form by adding it to your account.

The release of fat from its storage depot requires a signal from the various hormones which control fat release. These tell the fat-releasing enzymes to get on with the job. Fat cannot come out of fat cells by simply shaking or rubbing them, just as you cannot get your money out of a bank by walking straight in and taking it off the counter. There is a definite protocol for both. So the only time that fat will come out of your fat cells is when you need *more* energy than you are getting from food and drink. This is the *only* time that the hormones and enzymes will cause fat release from the storage forms into forms which your body can easily use to provide you with energy.

CHAPTER THREE

How To Choose Your Diet

BY 'EATING LESS' I mean consuming (i.e. eating and drinking) fewer calories, which as already explained, is your aim if you want to lose weight. This does not mean eating less in terms of weight or volume. It is sometimes possible to eat greater weights and volumes of food even though you are eating fewer calories. With just a little bit of knowledge about the composition of food you can make eating reasonably pleasant. The two commonest methods are (1) restricting calories *directly*, or (2) restricting calories *indirectly* by cutting down the amount of carbohydrates that you eat.

Calorie Cutting

The first method is the basic one. It simply means that you keep a check on the calorie values of the foods you eat and make certain that your total intake for the day is less than your output for that day. How much less will be the key factor in determining how much weight you lose and the speed at which you lose it.

When the way in which fat is formed was discussed above, I mentioned that each ounce of fat you eat provides you with about 250 Calories. It therefore follows that when an ounce of stored fat is broken down and released from the fat cells it will supply about 250 Calories of energy. So if you have a calorie deficit of about 250 Calories you will have to break down an ounce of pure fat. You will also lose the small amount of water associated with this fat and, on a larger scale, you need to have a deficit of about 3,500 Calories to lose a pound in weight. So if you are using up, on average, 2,000 Calories a day and you are taking in, on average, 1,500 Calories a day, your daily calorie deficit will be 500 Calories and you should lose a pound a week. In fact, during the first week of a diet, especially if you are overweight, you will lose weight at a faster rate than this because you are losing extra water from your body as well as fat. Unfortunately, after you have lost this excess fluid, you will then lose only fat, so your weight loss will seem to slow down. So do not get depressed when you lose less weight after the second and third week than you did after the first week.

If, of course, you want to lose your weight quicker, you can make your daily calorie deficit larger — say, 1,000 Calories. Then you would lose a pound of fat in four days. The factors you should consider when choosing your calorie limit are discussed later (page 19).

As far as making fat is concerned, *surplus* calories from *any* source are equally bad. Carbohydrates, fats and proteins can all be converted to fat and stored. However, when you are restricting the calories you have, you should bear in mind what has been said on pages 12 to 14. Proteins, vitamins and mineral salts are essential for good health. So, when you are having fewer calories, make certain that you still get enough of these essential nutrients in your daily allowance. If you reckon on having about half your allowance in foods which are very low in carbohydrate and rich in protein (e.g. meat, poultry, fish, eggs) you will not go far wrong.

Carbohydrate Cutting

In recent years, low carbohydrate diets have risen in popularity and, although many people have successfully lost a lot of weight on them, they have led to several misconceptions about the 'fattening potential' of different foods.

The strange thing is that the idea of a low carbohydrate diet is not a new one. As long ago as 1864, a Victorian undertaker by the name of William Banting published his *Letter on Corpulence* which he 'dedicated to the public simply and entirely from an earnest desire to confer a benefit on my fellow creatures'. After years of trying to reduce his fifteen-stone mass by means of steam baths, spas and exercise, he was eventually given some successful advice. This was to abstain from bread, butter, milk, sugar, beer and potatoes, which, as he put it, 'had been the main elements of my existence. . . .' By following this advice, Banting lost about a pound a week and had lost about 2½ stone when he wrote about his experiences. So, a new method of slimming, or 'banting' as it was then called, was born.

What is a low carbohydrate diet? Well, if you follow one you must cut right down on foods that contain a high proportion of starch or sugar, i.e. carbohydrate. This is *not* because, on a weight for weight basis, carbohydrates will make you any fatter than protein or fat. It is because:

● *Most people eat about half their daily calories in sugary or starchy foods. So it follows that cutting down on these should automatically reduce most people's total calorie intake.*
● *Carbohydrates very often act as 'carriers for fats', e.g. bread (carbohydrate) carries butter (fat). So if you cut down on carbohydrates you should find that the amount of fat you eat is less too.*

Nutritionally speaking, carbohydrates are the least important of the nutrients. Although you must have a certain amount every day – 50 gm., or 2 oz. is about right – it is much more important that you do not go without any essential proteins, minerals and vitamins.

As mentioned earlier, the popularity of low carbohydrate diets has resulted in some misconceptions. Bread, potatoes, sweets, pastry and ice cream, etc. are thought of as being terribly fattening, while bacon and eggs, grilled steak, avocado pears, etc. have a halo of goodness surrounding them and are thought of as 'slimming foods'. The truth is that *no* food is slimming – not even those which are completely free of carbohydrates. In fact, if you look at the food tables on pages 26 to 33, you will see that whereas potatoes contain 25 Calories an ounce, beef has 75 Calories an ounce. However, the carbohydrates in potatoes account for about 90 per cent of the solid matter (5·9 gm. per ounce) yet beef is completely free of carbohydrates.

If the diet is going to work properly, you must make sure that restricting carbohydrates is going to result in an *overall decrease* in the amount of food you eat. If you make up for the carbohydrates by overindulging in the carbohydrate free, yet high calorie foods, you certainly will *not* lose weight – you might even gain it.

Making the Choice

No doubt some of you have already tried various diets and can recognise from what has been said so far whether they are based on 'Cutting Down Calories' or 'Cutting Down Carbohydrates'. If so, you will have a good idea of how the method that you tried suited you. The choice between the two methods is very much a personal matter and largely depends on the kind of person you are, the type of life you lead and the sort of foods you like.

If you are not sure which method to try, I suggest you try the following quiz. Answer the questions truthfully and put a ring round the most applicable answer in either Column A or Column B.

	Column A	Column B
Do you normally eat a lot of starchy and sugary foods?	No	Yes
Would you find it difficult to cut right down on sweet and starchy foods or alcohol?	Yes	No
Are you a persistent nibbler?	Yes	No
Are you more than 2 stone overweight?	No	Yes
Is this the first time you have tried to lose weight?	No	Yes
Do you cook for yourself mainly?	Yes	No
Do you eat out a lot?	No	Yes
Have you lost a certain amount of weight but find it difficult to lose that last bit?	Yes	No
Do you like making reasonably accurate calculations about what you eat and drink?	Yes	No
Are you living on a somewhat limited budget?	Yes	No
Have you failed previously on other diets?	Yes	No

Now count up the number of answers you have ringed in both columns. If you have ringed most answers in Column A, then the method which involves cutting down on calories is recommended. If you have ringed more answers in Column B, you should start by cutting down on carbohydrates.

Your Daily Allowance

For calorie cutters

It has already been explained on page 16 how the amount of weight you lose depends on your 'calorie deficit' — the bigger your deficit the quicker you will lose weight. However, you have got to be sensible about this. It is no good practically starving yourself so that you have a calorie deficit of about 1,500 Calories but find it so unbearable that you can only keep it up for about a week. Much better to set yourself a target that you can keep up for the length of time that it will take you to get slim. Also, you will find it much easier to adapt your eating habits to a regime for 'staying slim'.

Setting your limit, then, will depend on two things:

    a. how much weight you want to lose and
    b. your average daily level of using up energy.

To help you decide which limit you should set yourself look at the following statements and mark which is most applicable in each group:

    *I want to lose 2 stone or more
    I want to lose less than 2 stone

    I sit down for most of the working day
    I sit down for about half the working day
    *I am on my feet for most of the working day
    *I regularly walk more than 2 miles a day

    *I am used to eating quite large meals
    The meals I have at present are not excessively large

If you have marked any of the asterisked statements, you should set a daily calorie limit of 1,500 Calories. Otherwise, you should be able to manage on a daily limit of 1,000 Calories.

For carbohydrate cutters

Those of you who have decided to cut down your carbohydrates could start by setting yourself a daily limit of 50 gm. of carbohydrate. The counting that you have to do has been kept down to a minimum by converting the carbohydrate values to a unit system (1 Carbohydrate Unit equals 5 gm. of carbohydrate). So all you have to do is to make certain that you have no more than 10 Carbohydrate Units (CH Units) a day. If you are a successful carbohydrate cutter you should find it easy to cut this down even further.

CHAPTER FOUR

Living With Your Diet

BY THIS TIME, you should have decided whether calorie cutting or carbo-hydrate cutting is to be the answer to your slimming problem. The theory behind both these methods has already been explained and so I shall now talk about how they work out in practice.

Tips for calorie cutters

When you have decided on your calorie limit of 1,000 or 1,500 Calories per day, at first you will probably need to keep on looking at the list of food and drink values on pages 26 to 34 to check the calorie value of the foods you want to eat. Since most of these values are given *per* ounce of food, you will also have to become aware of the actual *amount* of food that you are eating. Although this will take time to begin with, you will soon find that you get used to judging weights and knowing approximate calorie values. The calorie values in the tables are, in fact, only approximate to the nearest 5 Calories because it is difficult and pointless to make them more accurate.

The suggestion that you set your calorie allowance at 1,000 or 1,500, does not mean that you must eat exactly this number every day. It is best to plan on a *weekly basis* so that you end up having an average of 1,000 or 1,500 over the seven days. Try to work out what your average eating day would be. A normal weekday might consist of a cooked breakfast with the family in the morning, a light lunch and a larger evening meal. If so, work out how you can stick to this eating routine when restricting yourself to your calorie allowance. If you are used to having more meals at a weekend, say a larger lunch and afternoon tea as well as supper, you must take this into account. For example, you could plan a normal week as follows:

Monday	1,000 Calories
Tuesday	1,000 Calories
Wednesday	1,000 Calories
Thursday	700 Calories
Friday	700 Calories
Saturday	1,300 Calories
Sunday	1,300 Calories

Of course, very few of us ever have a 'normal week'. More often than not there will be some occasion during the week which will tempt you to exceed your allowance. If you know of such an occasion in advance, plan ahead for it and then you will be able to enjoy it as normal. Suppose you are invited to a wedding reception on Saturday afternoon, by cutting your calories right down during the week and on Saturday morning you can enjoy yourself there and might still lose weight.

Sometimes, however, these occasions crop up with no forewarning and these can be the most tempting of all to the slimmer – a sudden invitation to stay to supper when you are visiting friends, for example. Some of you may be strong willed enough to be able to restrict what you eat but those who are not so strong willed should use the technique of making up immediately after the event. So, if you know that you have gone way over your allowance on Saturday night, you must be extra good for the next day or so.

So far, I have talked about your daily calorie allowance but have not given any advice about how to spread these calories throughout the day. The reason for this is that it depends so much on the sort of life you lead. If you have always been used to a main meal at lunchtime and a small tea in the evening, you will want to have most of your calories at midday. If you have been used to large evening meals, you will want to plan your day so that you have got most of your calories left for the evening. If you are one of those people who never really has set meal times but tends to have several small snacks, you can still keep to your calorie allowance so long as you are aware of the number of calories you are eating at each of these. In fact, taking your food in a number of small snacks rather than one large meal is thought to be the best method of all for successful slimming.

Tips for carbohydrate cutters

If you are a carbohydrate cutter, you have a slightly easier job than calorie cutters when it comes to knowing which foods you should try to avoid. By putting the following foods into your strictly taboo list, you will not go far wrong:

   a. sugar and sugary foods like sweets and chocolate
   b. cakes, biscuits, pies, stodgy puddings and pastry
   c. potatoes, rice, flour and all forms of pasta
   d. bread, rolls and cereals
   e. sweet spreads like honey, jam and marmalade
   f. alcohol and soft drinks.

This still leaves you a good choice of carbohydrate-free foods, such as meat, poultry, fish, eggs, vegetables and fresh fruit, with which to make yourself good satisfying meals. Since carbohydrate cutting will only help you to lose weight if it results in you taking in less calories than you use up, you must stick to it earnestly to make it work. You cannot afford to cheat so much as calorie cutters and if you follow my advice you should find that you do not need to.

Look at the list of foods which are strictly taboo and visualise situations in your life when you are likely to be tempted by any of them. Then think of a way in which you can avoid this temptation or substitute something which is carbohydrate-free.

A lot of high carbohydrate foods tend to be eaten as snacks between meals –

chocolate bars, biscuits with morning coffee, cakes with afternoon tea, etc. Work out why you have these snacks. If you missed out morning coffee completely, would it be easier to resist the biscuits? Do you take a cake purely out of habit every time the plate is passed to you? In the face of temptation, it is a good idea to make yourself stop and think: 'Am I really going to enjoy this biscuit or am I just going to feel angry with myself and guilty when I've eaten it?'

Sugar substitutes will be discussed in a later section (page 40). Train yourself to take saccharin instead of sugar, or, alternatively, you can gradually train yourself to take your tea and coffee with less and less sugar. If, at the same time, you are giving up other sweet things, you will not find it too difficult.

As far as main course carbohydrates are concerned, there are plenty of ways in which you can avoid them. It is a pity that the traditional 'meat and two veg' nearly always means that one of the veg is potatoes. Although raw potatoes do not contain many calories or carbohydrates per ounce, they are usually served in quite large quantities of four ounces or more and quite often as chips or other forms involving cooking in fat. So it is best to avoid them completely and substitute one or two more vegetables instead. The same applies to rice and pasta.

Apart perhaps from roadside transport cafés which always seem to have menus as heavily laden with carbohydrates as the lorries that draw up outside, most cafés and restaurants have menus from which it is possible to pick a reasonably low carbohydrate meal. If you have a starter, go for the fruits like grapefruit, melon or avocados, or the salads rather than the soups or patés (you will not be so tempted by the rolls and toast). Then choose a really filling meat or fish course and have lots of vegetables and salads rather than potatoes or pasta. If you want anything to follow, choose fresh fruit or a light airy pudding such as mousse rather than pies and heavy puddings. If you choose carefully, your diet will not be ruined and no one will know that you are on one.

If you have a sudden unfortunate day when you eat quite a lot of high carbohydrate foods, the next day your weight will probably increase by a pound or two. This is due to a temporary fluid retention associated with the sudden change in your carbohydrate intake. As long as you return to strict carbohydrate cutting, your weight will soon go down.

The social acceptability of carbohydrate cutting makes it one of the most popular methods of dieting and for many people it is also the most successful. However, the fact that some people discover how easy it is to cut right down on carbohydrates if they eat much more of the protein and fat rich foods such as meat, fish, cheese and eggs, can sometimes lead to the failure of this diet. You must never forget that, whichever method you use, your aim is to take in less energy than you are using up.

Checking Your Progress

One of the best ways in which you can spur yourself on when you are trying to lose weight is to keep a graph of your weight loss. Decide right at the start when, where and how you are going to weigh yourself. If you have bathroom scales at home, your lightest weight can be measured if you weigh yourself naked first thing in the morning after you have been to the toilet and before breakfast. There is no need to weigh yourself every day — three times a week is ample. If you do not have your own scales, reliable, accurate scales can be found at Boots. Wear the same clothes every time you step on the scales and try to weigh yourself at the same time of the day. The chart on page 24 is for you to plot your weight. An example is shown below. Fill in the vertical scale so that your starting weight is reasonably near the top. Mark in the weight you want to reach with a red line so that you can never forget your target. The horizontal line records individual days and weeks, up to four months. Every time you weigh yourself put a cross on the graph in the appropriate place. Join up the crosses and you will see your weight loss. After you have been dieting for about three or four weeks, you will be able to get a rough estimate of when you will reach your target. Ignore the slope of the line for the first and second weeks and extend the slope of the line for the third and fourth weeks (dotted line). The point at which this extended line hits the original red 'target' line will give you some idea of when you should reach your target.

Keeping Daily Records

If you really want to know what you are eating in the way of calories and CH Units, try to keep a daily eating record. The chart on page 25 is an example of a calorie cutter's record. By examining your chart at the end of the day you will often see where you could have cut down if your limit has been over-stepped. This method will also help you to learn the calorie and CH content of the foods you eat most often.

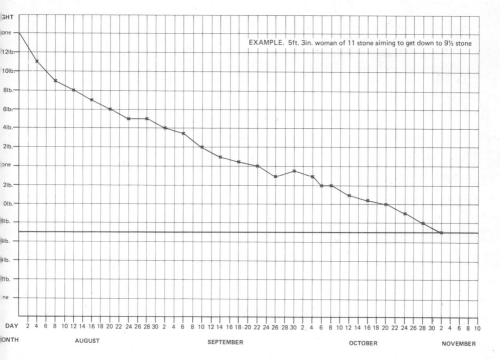

EXAMPLE. 5ft. 3in. woman of 11 stone aiming to get down to 9½ stone

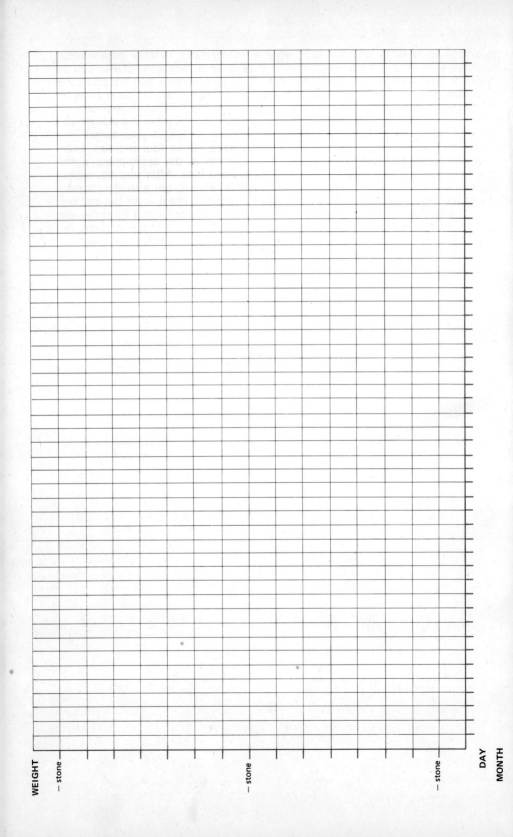

WEIGHT

— stone

— stone

— stone

DAY

MONTH

Calorie Cutter's Chart

Date: Monday. February 5th		Calories
Breakfast	Boiled egg	90
	2 pieces of buttered toast	200
	Cup of tea, no sugar	20
Mid morning	Cup of milky coffee (1 teaspoonful sugar)	150
Lunch	3 oz. lean ham	180
	1 tomato	10
	Lettuce	5
	1 medium apple	40
Mid afternoon	Cup of tea, no sugar	20
	Small sweet biscuit	80
Supper	8 oz. grilled plaice	120
	3 oz. frozen peas	60
	3 oz. new potatoes	75
	Glass of dry sherry	55
Late evening	Cup of cocoa, made with all milk (1 teaspoon sugar)	170
		1,275

Verdict:
1. Replace mid morning coffee by tea.   Saving: 130 Calories
2. Only have one piece of toast for breakfast.   Saving: 100 Calories

Total saving: 230 Calories

CHAPTER FIVE

Food Value Tables

NOTES

1. All calorie values are to the nearest 5 Calories.
2. 1 Carbohydrate Unit (CH Unit) is equivalent to 5 gm. carbohydrate. CH Units given to nearest $\frac{1}{2}$ Unit (except where it is below $\frac{1}{2}$ CH Unit where $\frac{1}{4}$ Unit is given if necessary).
3. In the case of alcoholic drinks, the weight of alcohol has been converted to the equivalent weight of carbohydrate to calculate the true CH Unit value.
4. All weights should be taken as *total* weights as bought even if certain parts are inedible (unless otherwise stated), e.g.
   weight for apple includes core and pips
   weight for olives includes stones
   weight for hake includes bones and skin.
5. As far as possible, food values are given for *raw* foodstuffs. This is because the cooking method is very important in determining the total calorie value of the food when you eat it (see 'Cooking Methods for Slimmers', page 42).
6. Values are given for lean meat only. Any fat will increase calorie content.
7. All food values are derived from *The Composition of Foods*, by R. A. McCance and E. M. Widdowson (HMSO, 1960).

FOOD	PORTION	CALORIES	CH UNITS
Anchovies	1 oz. (6 fillets)	40	0
Apples	1 oz.	10	$\frac{1}{2}$
	1 medium (4 oz.)	40	2
Apricots, fresh	1 oz. (1 medium)	5	$\frac{1}{4}$
canned in syrup	1 oz. (1 medium)	30	$1\frac{1}{2}$
dried	1 oz.	50	$2\frac{1}{2}$
Arrowroot	1 oz.	100	5
Artichokes, Globe, raw	1 oz.	5	0
Jerusalem, raw	1 oz.	5	0
Asparagus, raw	1 oz.	5	0
Aubergines, raw	1 oz.	5	0
Avocado pears, raw	1 oz.	25	0
	1 medium (10 oz.)	250	$\frac{1}{2}$
Bacon, lean, streaky, raw	1 oz.	115	0
gammon, raw	1 oz.	90	0

FOOD	PORTION	CALORIES	CH UNITS
Bananas, raw	1 oz.	15	$\frac{1}{2}$
	1 medium (4 oz.)	60	2
Barley, raw	1 oz.	100	$4\frac{1}{2}$
boiled	1 oz.	35	$1\frac{1}{2}$
Bass, steamed	1 oz.	20	0
Beans, baked	1 oz.	25	1
broad, raw	1 oz.	10	$\frac{1}{2}$
butter, raw	1 oz.	75	3
haricot, raw	1 oz.	75	$2\frac{1}{2}$
runner, raw	1 oz.	5	0
Beef, very lean only, raw	1 oz.	75	0
Beetroot, raw	1 oz.	10	$\frac{1}{4}$
Biscuits, plain	1 oz. (2 biscuits)	125	4
sweet	1 oz. (2 biscuits)	160	4
Blackberries, raw	1 oz.	10	$\frac{1}{4}$
Blackcurrants, raw	1 oz.	10	$\frac{1}{4}$
Bloaters, raw	1 oz.	40	0
Brains, raw	1 oz.	30	0
Bread, white or brown	1 oz.	70	3
	average slice large loaf	80	$3\frac{1}{2}$
	average slice small loaf	50	2
malt	1 oz.	70	3
currant	1 oz.	70	3
Broccoli, raw	1 oz.	5	0
Brussels Sprouts, raw	1 oz.	10	$\frac{1}{4}$
Butter	1 oz.	225	0
Buttermilk	1 pint	235	$5\frac{1}{2}$
Cabbage, raw, red or white	1 oz.	5	$\frac{1}{4}$
Cake, plain fruit	1 oz.	105	3
rich fruit, e.g. Dundee	1 oz.	110	$3\frac{1}{2}$
sponge	1 oz.	85	3
Carrots, raw	1 oz.	5	$\frac{1}{4}$
Cauliflower, raw	1 oz.	5	$\frac{1}{4}$
Celery, raw	1 oz.	3	0
Cheese, Austrian smoked	1 oz.	80	0
Caerphilly	1 oz.	100	0
Camembert	1 oz.	90	0
Cheddar	1 oz.	120	0
Cheshire	1 oz.	110	0
Cottage	1 oz.	30	0
Cream	1 oz.	230	0
Curd	1 oz.	40	0
Danish Blue	1 oz.	105	0
Edam	1 oz.	90	0
Finnish loaf	1 oz.	95	0
Gorgonzola	1 oz.	110	0
Gouda	1 oz.	95	0
Gruyère	1 oz.	130	0

FOOD	PORTION	CALORIES	CH UNITS
Jarlsberg	1 oz.	95	0
Leicester	1 oz.	110	0
Norwegian Mysost	1 oz.	135	2
Parmesan	1 oz.	120	0
Processed	1 oz.	105	0
Roquefort	1 oz.	90	0
Spread	1 oz.	80	0
Stilton	1 oz.	135	0
Wensleydale	1 oz.	115	0
Cherries, fresh	1 oz.	10	$\frac{1}{2}$
glacé	1 oz.	60	3
Chicken, flesh only, raw	1 oz.	35	0
Chicory, raw	1 oz.	3	0
Chives, raw	1 oz.	10	0
Chocolate, milk	1 oz.	165	3
plain	1 oz.	155	3
Chutney, apple	1 oz.	55	3
Cockles, flesh only, raw	1 oz.	15	0
Cod, raw	1 oz.	20	0
Cod roe, raw	1 oz.	35	0
Corn on the Cob, raw	1 oz.	30	1
	1 medium (4 oz.)	85	4
Cornflakes, and most cereals	1 oz.	105	5
Cornflour	1 oz.	100	5
Courgettes, raw	1 oz.	2	0
Crab, meat only, boiled	1 oz.	35	0
Cranberries, raw	1 oz.	5	$\frac{1}{4}$
Cranberry sauce	1 oz. (1 tablespoon)	60	$2\frac{1}{2}$
Cream, double	1 oz. (2 tablespoons)	130	$\frac{1}{4}$
single	1 oz. (2 tablespoons)	60	$\frac{1}{4}$
soured	1 oz. (2 tablespoons)	55	$\frac{1}{4}$
canned	1 oz. (2 tablespoons)	70	$\frac{1}{4}$
Cucumber, raw	1 oz.	3	0
Currants	1 oz.	70	$3\frac{1}{2}$
Custard powder	1 oz.	100	5
Damsons, raw	1 oz.	10	$\frac{1}{2}$
Dates	1 oz.	60	3
Dripping, beef	1 oz.	260	0
Duck, meat only, raw	1 oz.	70	0
Dumplings	1 oz.	60	$1\frac{1}{2}$
Eel, raw	1 oz.	60	0
meat only, cooked	1 oz.	105	0
Eggs, whole	1 small	70	0
	1 standard	80	0
	1 large	90	0
whole	1 oz.	45	0
white	1 oz.	10	0
yolk	1 oz.	100	0

FOOD	PORTION	CALORIES	CH UNITS
Figs, fresh, green	1 oz.	10	$\frac{1}{2}$
dried	1 oz.	60	3
Flounder, raw	1 oz.	15	0
Flour	1 oz.	100	5
Garlic	1 clove	2	0
Gelatine powder	1 oz. (8 level teaspoons)	100	0
Goose, meat only, raw	1 oz.	70	0
Gooseberries, raw	1 oz.	10	$\frac{1}{2}$
Grapefruit, flesh only, raw	1 oz.	5	$\frac{1}{4}$
whole fruit	1 medium (4 oz.)	30	$1\frac{1}{2}$
Grapes, black or white	1 oz.	15	1
Gravy mix	1 oz. (3 teaspoons)	25	$1\frac{1}{4}$
Greengages	1 oz.	15	$\frac{1}{2}$
Grouse, meat only, roast	1 oz.	35	0
Haddock, white, raw	1 oz.	20	0
smoked, raw	1 oz.	20	0
Hake, fillets only, raw	1 oz.	25	0
Halibut, raw	1 oz.	30	0
Ham, York, raw	1 oz.	145	0
lean only, boiled	1 oz.	60	0
Heart, raw	1 oz.	30–45	0
Herring, raw	1 oz.	65	0
Honey	1 oz.	80	4
Horseradish sauce	1 oz. (1 tablespoon)	10	$\frac{1}{2}$
Ice cream	1 oz.	55	1
Icing, glacé	1 oz.	105	5
Jam	1 oz.	75	4
Jelly, made up	1 pint	420	$19\frac{1}{2}$
cubes	1 oz.	75	$3\frac{1}{2}$
Kidney, raw	1 oz.	30–35	0
Kippers, raw	1 oz.	30	0
Lamb, very lean only, raw	1 oz.	75	0
Lard	1 oz.	260	0
Leeks, raw	1 oz.	10	$\frac{1}{4}$
Lemon, raw	1 oz.	5	0
Lemon curd	1 oz.	85	$2\frac{1}{2}$
Lemon juice	1 fl. oz. (2 tablespoons)	2	0
Lentils, raw	1 oz.	85	3
Lettuce, raw	1 oz.	3	0
Liver, raw	1 oz.	40–45	0

FOOD	PORTION	CALORIES	CH UNITS
Liver sausage, raw	1 oz.	90	1
Lobster, whole, raw	1 oz.	10	0
flesh only, raw	1 oz,	35	0
Loganberries, raw	1 oz.	5	$\frac{1}{4}$
Macaroni, raw	1 oz.	100	$4\frac{1}{2}$
boiled	1 oz.	30	$1\frac{1}{2}$
Mackerel, raw	1 oz.	30	0
Margarine	1 oz.	225	0
Marmalade	1 oz.	75	4
Marrow, boiled	1 oz.	2	0
Melon	1 oz.	5	$\frac{1}{4}$
Milk, whole	1 fl. oz.	20	$\frac{1}{4}$
	1 pint	380	$5\frac{1}{2}$
separated	1 pint	190	$5\frac{1}{2}$
made from low fat skimmed powder	1 pint	190	$5\frac{1}{2}$
Mincemeat	1 oz.	35	$1\frac{1}{2}$
Mint, raw	1 oz. (2 tablespoons)	2	0
Mushrooms, raw	1 oz.	2	0
Mussels, flesh only, raw	1 oz.	20	0
Mustard and cress	1 oz.	3	0
Mustard, made up	1 oz. (1 tablespoon)	10	0
dry	1 oz. (3 teaspoons)	130	1
Nuts, almonds, shelled, raw	1 oz.	170	$\frac{1}{4}$
brazils, shelled, raw	1 oz.	180	$\frac{1}{4}$
chestnuts, shelled, raw	1 oz.	50	2
cob, shelled, raw	1 oz.	115	$\frac{1}{4}$
coconut, shelled, raw	1 oz.	105	$\frac{1}{4}$
peanuts, shelled, raw	1 oz.	170	$\frac{1}{2}$
peanuts, roast and salted	1 oz.	180	$\frac{1}{2}$
walnuts, shelled, raw	1 oz.	155	$\frac{1}{4}$
Oatmeal, raw	1 oz.	115	4
Oil, olive or corn	1 fl. oz.	265	0
Olives, raw	1 oz. (about 8–10)	25	0
Onions, raw	1 oz.	5	$\frac{1}{4}$
Oranges, raw	1 oz.	10	$\frac{1}{4}$
	1 medium	40	$2\frac{1}{2}$
Oxtail, joints on bone	1 oz.	40	0
Oysters, shelled, raw	1 oz.	15	0
Parsley	1 oz.	5	0
Parsnips, raw	1 oz.	15	$\frac{1}{2}$
Pastry, short, baked	1 oz.	155	3
flaky, baked	1 oz.	165	$2\frac{1}{2}$
Peaches, raw	1 oz.	10	$\frac{1}{2}$
	1 medium (4 oz.)	40	2

FOOD	PORTION	CALORIES	CH UNITS
Peanut butter	1 oz.	180	1
Pears, raw	1 oz.	10	$\frac{1}{2}$
	1 medium (4 oz.)	40	2
Peas, fresh or frozen, raw	1 oz.	20	$\frac{1}{2}$
canned, raw	1 oz.	25	1
Peppers, red or green, raw	1 oz.	10	0
Pickles, sweet	1 oz.	35	1
Pigeon, meat only, raw	1 oz.	60	0
Pilchards, canned, fish only	1 oz.	55	0
Pineapple, raw	1 oz.	15	$\frac{1}{2}$
canned with syrup	1 oz.	20	1
Plaice, raw	1 oz.	15	0
Plums, dessert, raw	1 oz.	10	$\frac{1}{2}$
Pork, very lean only, raw	1 oz.	35	0
Porridge, oatmeal, made up	1 oz.	15	$\frac{1}{2}$
Potatoes, raw	1 oz.	25	1
instant powder	1 oz. (1 tablespoon)	105	$4\frac{1}{2}$
Potato crisps	1 oz.	160	3
Prawns, whole, raw	1 oz.	10	0
flesh only, raw	1 oz.	30	0
Prunes, raw	1 oz.	40	2
Rabbit, meat only, raw	1 oz.	50	0
Radishes, raw	1 oz.	5	$\frac{1}{4}$
Raisins	1 oz.	70	$3\frac{1}{2}$
Raspberries, raw	1 oz.	5	$\frac{1}{4}$
Redcurrants, raw	1 oz.	5	$\frac{1}{4}$
Rhubarb, raw	1 oz.	2	0
Rice, raw	1 oz.	100	5
boiled	1 oz.	35	$1\frac{1}{2}$
Rolls, bread	1 oz.	70	3
Sago	1 oz.	100	5
Salad cream	1 oz. (2 tablespoons)	110	$\frac{1}{2}$
Salmon, fresh, raw	1 oz.	55	0
canned	1 oz.	40	0
smoked	1 oz.	35	0
Sardines, canned, fish only	1 oz.	85	0
Sausage, average, raw	1 oz.	100	1
(sausages vary greatly in composition)			
Scallops, steamed	1 oz.	30	0
Scampi, fried in batter	1 oz.	85	4
Semolina	1 oz.	100	$4\frac{1}{2}$
Shortbread	1 oz.	150	$3\frac{1}{2}$
Shrimps, flesh only	1 oz.	30	0
Sole, raw	1 oz.	15	0
Soup, clear, e.g. consommé, made up	$\frac{1}{2}$ pint	40–65	0–1
thin, e.g. chicken noodle, made up	$\frac{1}{2}$ pint	65–100	1–2

FOOD	PORTION	CALORIES	CH UNITS
thick, e.g. asparagus, made up	½ pint	90–200	2–6
(N.B. Packet soups are usually less fattening than canned soups)			
Spaghetti, raw	1 oz.	105	4½
boiled	1 oz.	35	1
canned in tomato sauce	1 oz.	15	½
Spinach, raw	1 oz.	5	0
Sprats, grilled	1 oz.	80	0
Spring greens, raw	1 oz.	3	0
Stock cube	each	15	½
Strawberries, raw	1 oz.	5	¼
Stuffing, sage and onion, etc. dry mixture	1 oz.	25	¾
Sturgeon, raw	1 oz.	30	0
Suet	1 oz.	260	0
Sugar, white or brown	1 oz. (1 tablespoon)	110	6
Sultanas	1 oz.	70	3½
Swedes, raw	1 oz.	5	¼
Sweets, boiled	1 oz.	95	5
Sweetbreads, stewed	1 oz.	50	0
Sweetcorn, canned or frozen	1 oz.	25	1
Syrup	1 oz.	85	4½
Tangerines	1 oz.	5	¼
	1 medium (4 oz.)	20	1
Tomatoes, raw	1 oz.	5	¼
	1 medium (2 oz.)	10	½
Tomato purée	1 oz. (2 tablespoons)	40	2
Tongue	1 oz.	85	0
Treacle, black	1 oz.	75	4
Tripe, stewed	1 oz.	30	0
Trout, raw	1 oz.	25	0
Tuna, canned in oil	1 oz.	75	0
Turbot, raw	1 oz.	20	0
Turkey, meat only, raw	1 oz.	35	0
Turnips, raw	1 oz.	5	¼
Veal, fillet, raw	1 oz.	30	0
Vinegar	1 oz. (2 tablespoons)	1	0
Watercress	1 oz.	5	0
Whelks, flesh only, raw	1 oz.	25	0
Whiting, raw	1 oz.	15	0
Winkles, flesh only, boiled	1 oz.	25	0

FOOD	PORTION	CALORIES	CH UNITS
Yoghurt, plain, low fat	1 fl. oz.	15	$\frac{1}{4}$
	average 5 oz. carton	75	$1\frac{1}{4}$
fruit flavoured	1 fl. oz.	25	1
	average 5 oz. carton	125	5
Yorkshire pudding	1 oz.	65	$1\frac{1}{2}$

ALCOHOLIC DRINKS	QUANTITY	CALORIES	CH UNITS
Beer, brown ale	1 pint	160	8
draught bitter	1 pint	180	$8\frac{1}{2}$
draught mild	1 pint	140	7
lager	1 pint	150	$7\frac{1}{2}$
pale ale	1 pint	180	9
stout, bottled	1 pint	200	$10\frac{1}{2}$
strong ale	$\frac{1}{3}$ pint	140	$6\frac{1}{2}$
Brandy	standard pub glass ($\frac{1}{6}$ gill)	75	4
Bourbon	standard pub glass ($\frac{1}{6}$ gill)	65	3
Campari	standard pub glass ($\frac{1}{3}$ gill)	120	6
Cider, dry	1 pint	200	$10\frac{1}{2}$
sweet	1 pint	240	$12\frac{1}{2}$
Cocktails	varies according to ingredients	115–300	$5\frac{1}{2}$–15
Gin	standard pub glass ($\frac{1}{6}$ gill)	55	$2\frac{1}{2}$
Liqueurs	varies according to type, liqueur glass	65–90	$3–4\frac{1}{2}$
Port	standard pub glass ($\frac{1}{3}$ gill)	75	4
Rum	standard pub glass ($\frac{1}{6}$ gill)	75	4
Shandy	$11\frac{1}{2}$ fl. oz. can	115	$5\frac{1}{2}$
Sherry, dry	standard pub glass ($\frac{1}{3}$ gill)	55	3
sweet	standard pub glass ($\frac{1}{3}$ gill)	65	3
Vermouth, dry	standard pub glass ($\frac{1}{3}$ gill)	55	3
sweet	standard pub glass ($\frac{1}{3}$ gill)	75	4
Vodka	standard pub glass ($\frac{1}{6}$ gill)	65	3
Whisky	standard pub glass ($\frac{1}{6}$ gill)	60	3
Wine, dry	medium glass (4·4 fl. oz.)	90	5
sweet	medium glass (4·4 fl. oz.)	115	$5\frac{1}{2}$

SOFT DRINKS	QUANTITY	CALORIES	CH UNITS
Apple juice, unsweetened	small glass	50	$2\frac{1}{2}$
Bitter lemon	$11\frac{1}{2}$ fl. oz. can	110	$5\frac{1}{2}$
Blackcurrant concentrate	1 tablespoon	35	2
Carrot juice	small glass	25	1
Cola	$11\frac{1}{2}$ fl. oz. can	125	$6\frac{1}{2}$
Dry ginger	$11\frac{1}{2}$ fl. oz. can	50	$2\frac{1}{2}$
Grapefruit juice, unsweetened	small glass	55	3
Grapefruit concentrate	2 tablespoons	35	2
Lemon juice, unsweetened	small glass	10	$\frac{1}{2}$
Lemon concentrate	2 tablespoons	35	2
Lemonade, aerated	1 pint	120	$6\frac{1}{2}$
Lime juice concentrate	2 tablespoons	30	2
Lucozade	small glass	105	$5\frac{1}{2}$
Orange juice, unsweetened	small glass	60	3
Orange concentrate	2 tablespoons	40	2
Pineapple juice, unsweetened	small glass	70	$3\frac{1}{2}$
Tomato juice	small glass	25	1
Tonic water	$11\frac{1}{2}$ fl. oz. can	90	$4\frac{1}{2}$

MILKY DRINKS	QUANTITY	CALORIES	CH UNITS
Cocoa, powder	1 oz. (2 tablespoons)	130	2
drink made with all milk	cup (6 fl. oz.)	135	2
Coffee, powder	1 oz. (2 tablespoons)	25	$\frac{1}{2}$
black, no sugar	cup	negligible	
drink made with all milk	cup (6 fl. oz.)	115	$1\frac{1}{2}$
Malted drinks (e.g. Bournvita, Ovaltine) made with all milk	cup (6 fl. oz.)	165	$3\frac{1}{2}$
Milk, fresh whole	1 pint	380	$5\frac{1}{2}$
separated	1 pint	190	$5\frac{1}{2}$
made from low fat powder	1 pint	190	$5\frac{1}{2}$
evaporated	2 tablespoons	45	$\frac{1}{2}$
condensed, sweetened	2 tablespoons	100	3
Tea, black, no sugar	cup	negligible	
drink made with 2 tablespoons milk	cup (6 fl. oz.)	20	$\frac{1}{4}$

SAVOURY DRINKS	QUANTITY	CALORIES	CH UNITS
Bovril	cup made with 1 teaspoon	5	0
Marmite	cup made with 1 teaspoon	10	0
Oxo	cup made with 1 cube	15	$\frac{1}{2}$

CHAPTER SIX

Choosing what to Eat and Drink

THE FOOD VALUE TABLES on the previous pages tell you how many calories and how many CH Units different foods contain. In this chapter, I want to draw your attention to some points which should be considered when you, as a slimmer, go out shopping.

Meat, Offal and Poultry

If you are going to be a carbohydrate cutter, all types of meat can be considered as free of carbohydrates and so, theoretically, you can eat as much as you like.

If you are a calorie cutter, it is a good idea to include lots of offal and poultry in your shopping list because these are less fatty (and cheaper) than beef, pork and lamb and you can get much more lean meat for the same number of calories. You can see this for yourself in the following table which lists the amounts of protein and fat commonly found in 100 Calories worth of the different types of raw meat:

	protein (gm.)	fat (gm.)
Chicken	14·4	4·7
Kidney	16·1	4·0
Liver	11·9	5·8
Beef	4·7	9·0
Lamb	3·9	9·4
Pork	2·9	9·8

The less usual forms of offal such as tripe, sweetbreads, hearts and brains are also comparatively low in calories, so be adventurous and experiment with some of these.

Although beef, as you buy it in the shop, is slightly less fatty than lamb and pork, once you have taken off all the visible fat from these meats before eating there is not much difference. Another thing to remember is that you do not have to buy the most expensive top quality steaks when you are slimming –

35

the price of meat is usually related more to its tenderness than its fat content (young animals giving the most tender meat). The tougher cuts of meat simply need longer cooking times by such methods as braising.

Fish

Fish is another food that carbohydrate cutters can eat freely because all types of raw fish are carbohydrate-free. But do not forget that you must cook it in a carbohydrate-free way – no thick batters are allowed (see page 75).

Calorie cutters should also try to include a lot of fish in their diet since it is a good source of protein and low in calories. White fish (cod, haddock, plaice, turbot, halibut, etc.) is less fatty and therefore lower in calories than oily fish (herrings, kippers, sardines, pilchards, sprats, etc.) so you should have smaller quantities of the oily group. All types of shellfish are very low in calories and therefore well worth including if you can afford them.

If you buy your fish in frozen packs, you should avoid the ones where the fish is already coated in batter or served in a thick sauce. The plain fillets or steaks are your best buy. Fish fingers and fish cakes, to a lesser extent, are also comparatively low in calories and make a good quick snack.

Eggs, Milk, Cheese and Fats

Eggs are one of the most useful of foods to any slimmer. Apart from being carbohydrate-free (carbohydrate cutters please note) and an excellent source of protein, vitamins and minerals, they are extremely versatile and can be cooked in many ways for many occasions (see page 92). Note that there is no difference whatsoever in the calorie content of brown, white, free range and battery produced eggs.

A pint of *milk* from your milkman contains about 380 Calories and $5\frac{1}{2}$ CH Units (about 240 Calories if you take off the cream). If you have extra creamy milk, e.g. Gold Top, the value will be higher – about 490 Calories. There is very little difference calorie-wise between goats' milk and cows' milk.

If you make up a pint of milk from one of the *low-fat skimmed powders*, you will reduce the calories to about 190 (but not the carbohydrates since 'skimming' means removing fat only). Calorie cutters could find it very worthwhile to buy these low-fat milk powders. They are especially useful for adding to drinks and making sauces where it is very difficult to tell the difference between them and the real thing. Some dairies now produce *separated milk* which also has about half the calories of ordinary milk so you could try this too.

Cream is a good example of a food which has caused much confusion amongst slimmers in the past. Single cream at 60 Calories an ounce and double cream at 130 Calories an ounce are certainly pretty high in calories and usually put on the forbidden list for calorie cutters. However, both contain comparatively little carbohydrate and so could, in theory, be eaten freely if you are cutting carbohydrate. Having already explained that the carbohydrate cutting method is really only an indirect calorie cutting method, I think those following it will understand why I advise steering clear of such high fat, high calorie foods as cream, even though the carbohydrate content is low. What can be used instead of cream? Well, ice cream is not a bad idea. An ounce of ice cream contains about 55 Calories and 1 CH Unit and will make a more filling sweet than adding an ounce of double cream. Ice cream, you see, contains more water and air than cream and neither of these contain calories or carbohydrates. Anything with a lot of air in it is, in fact, a good replacement for cream – an average portion of mousse, for example, will be about 55 Calories and 2 CH Units.

Yoghurt is another food which can be very useful for slimmers. It can be eaten by itself as a sweet (only about 75 Calories for an average sized carton of natural yoghurt but rising to about 125 Calories for the fruit flavoured ones) and natural yoghurt can be used instead of cream in certain savoury dishes and sauces.

Butter and margarine (in fact, all fats and oils) are all very high in calories (well over 200 an ounce), even though they are all carbohydrate-free. So the same warning applies to the carbohydrate cutters as before – do not overdo your fat consumption or you will not lose weight. Calorie cutters can replace butter and margarine completely by using the low-fat spread 'Outline' which has only half the calories. You can either use this as a spread or put a little on vegetables after cooking. Another method of cutting down on butter is to put other low calorie spreads *directly* on your bread, toast or biscuits – cottage or curd cheese, fish or meat paste, for example.

By the way, there is no difference in the calorie values of saturated and unsaturated fats, animal or vegetable fats. As far as slimmers are concerned, they are all just as fattening.

Cheese is yet another food which is carbohydrate-free. It is probably the food which causes the most downfalls among carbohydrate cutters. An ounce of ordinary hard cheese (and that is not a very big lump) contains about 100 Calories. So, my advice to carbohydrate cutters is to use cheese in their main meals by all means but not to nibble at it whenever they feel peckish.

Calorie cutters should try cottage and curd cheese, if they have not done so already, because at 30 and 40 Calories an ounce they represent quite a saving. You can use them both directly as a spread or in salads.

The hard cheeses are all very high in their calorie contents (they are all between 80 and 140 an ounce). Dutch cheeses are usually at the lower end of the scale as they are made from skimmed milk.

When eating any of the hard cheeses, grate them up and eat with a fork. The bulk this produces is at least psychologically, if not biologically, satisfying and discourages nibbling.

The only cheese you should avoid like the plague because it is fantastically calorific is cream cheese, which has 230 Calories an ounce – about the same as butter.

Fruit and Vegetables

On the whole, most fresh fruits and vegetables contain a lot of water and this is why they are all reasonably low in calories.

If you look at the figures given in the tables on pages 26 to 33 for apricots you will see the difference between fresh, canned and dried apricots. The calorie value for an ounce jumps from 5 to 30 to 50 and the CH Units are $\frac{1}{4}$, $1\frac{1}{2}$ and $2\frac{1}{2}$ respectively. The same pattern occurs with most fruits, the moral being to eat fresh fruit if at all possible.

If you want to remember which vegetables you should eat when you are slimming, think of how they are grown. As a general rule, leaf and stem vegetables (e.g. lettuce, cabbage) which are grown above the ground are less calorific than root vegetables which grow underground. Because these represent the plant's food store, they have quite a lot of starch and therefore more CH Units (e.g. carrots, potatoes).

A special word here about potatoes. Potatoes themselves are not nearly so fattening as a lot of people think, for about four-fifths of the potato is water. They only become very fattening if they are cooked in fattening ways. The following table shows how the way potatoes are cooked affects their calorie and carbohydrate values:

		Calories	CH. Units
Boiled potatoes	1 oz.	25	1
Baked potatoes	1 oz.	30	$1\frac{1}{2}$
Mashed potatoes	1 oz.	35	1
Roast potatoes	1 oz.	35	$1\frac{1}{2}$
Fried (chips, etc.)	1 oz.	70	2
Potato crisps	1 oz.	160	3

So if you boil or bake a medium sized potato (about 3 oz.) it will contain 75 or 90 Calories and 3 or $4\frac{1}{2}$ CH Units. But, if you chop it up and deep fry it as chips, the value jumps to 210 Calories and 6 CH Units. And note that a small 1 oz. bag of crisps which can be eaten quite absentmindedly will cost you about 160 Calories. If you use instant powdered potato, this will have about the same number of calories when made up as an equal weight of ordinary mashed potato.

Provided you cook your vegetables by methods that do not alter their nutritional content or fattening content (see page 112), you can really go to town on vegetables. Not only will they fill up your plate, which is good for you psychologically, but they should also fill *you* up. I have given some slightly more unusual methods of cooking vegetables and preparing salads in the recipe section.

Bread, Biscuits and Cakes

One thing that slimmers often find most difficult to cut down on is bread. Some of course can resist bread until it is toasted — but unfortunately toast is no less fattening than bread. So, if you do eat a lot of calories or carbo-hydrates in bread, what is the best way of cutting this down? Well, the easiest way is to cut down the number of slices of bread you eat every day. (By the way, there is no difference in calorie value between white and brown bread.) If you do not want to do this, you might consider buying some sort of bread substitute. There are two main types of bread for slimmers:

- *Some of the breads (Nimble, Wisp, Procea) are just 'lighter' than ordinary bread — more air, less bread. So, although an ounce of one of these breads is just as fattening as an ounce of real bread, the idea is that a normal sized* slice *from one of these breads contains less*

ounces and therefore less calories than real bread.
- *Some of the breads (e.g. St. Michael, Slimcea) are not only lighter but they have more protein and slightly less starch than real bread. Cambridge Formula loaf is particularly low in starch and therefore good for carbohydrate cutters.*

It is certainly worth trying these lighter breads. If you replace ordinary bread by the same number of slices of a lighter bread, you will automatically reduce your calories and carbohydrates by about a half.

Crispbreads are really just a concentrated form of bread which has had a lot of water removed. If you like them and want to include them in your diet instead of bread, it is definitely worth shopping around for those which are lowest in calories. The ones which are very low (usually under 30 per crispbread) are almost bound to have the value marked on the packet. The only crispbreads with a lower starch content for carbohydrate cutters are those which are actually marked 'starch reduced'. This means that they are less than 50 per cent starch. As long as you replace one piece of bread by one piece of crispbread and do not spread twice as much butter on it, you will save about 40 Calories per slice.

Unfortunately most biscuits and cakes have to be regarded as a real luxury by calorie and carbohydrate cutters alike. Their main ingredients are sugar, fat and flour – three very deadly foods for slimmers. If you really cannot do without biscuits or cakes – and you can crave for something sweet at times – try to stick to the plainest biscuits and cakes. A chocolate digestive biscuit contains about 40 Calories more than a plain digestive biscuit. Sponge cakes, particularly fatless ones, are better than fruit cakes because these contain additional calories and carbohydrates from all that dried fruit.

Sweets and Puddings

Some ideas for low calorie desserts are given in the Recipe Section on page 144. However, if you shop carefully you can buy several ready-made sweets which are reasonably low in calories, e.g. mousses, yoghurts and jellies.

One of the easiest sweets to prepare, of course, is fresh fruit. You cannot go very wrong with any fruit – oranges, apples, pears and peaches are all about 40 Calories and 2 CH Units each. Those fruits which have the highest water content usually have the lowest calorie and CH values as the following table shows:

Fresh fruits as bought	Water content (% whole fruit)	Calories per ounce whole fruit	CH Units per ounce whole fruit
Apples	85	10	$\frac{1}{2}$
Bananas	71	15	$\frac{1}{2}$
Gooseberries	90	10	$\frac{1}{2}$
Grapes	85	15	1
Lemons	91	5	0
Oranges	87	10	$\frac{1}{4}$
Pears	84	10	$\frac{1}{2}$
Plums	87	10	$\frac{1}{2}$
Raspberries	87	5	$\frac{1}{4}$
Rhubarb	98	2	0
Strawberries	90	5	$\frac{1}{4}$

Apart from their dissolved sugars and pectins, their value as foodstuffs lies mainly in their minerals and vitamins. Blackcurrants and oranges are particularly rich in Vitamin C; apricots, peaches and tomatoes in Vitamins A and B.

Most fruits which are usually stewed need sweetening and a few tablespoons of sugar could turn a low calorie sweet into a very high calorie one. Liquid sweeteners, like liquid Sweetex, can be useful here. Add the sweetener *after* you have stewed the fruit.

Sugar

Many would-be slimmers find that having a 'sweet tooth' is a serious drawback to their slimming attempts. After all, at 110 Calories and 6 CH Units an ounce, a spoonful of sugar might help the medicine go down but it certainly will not do the same for your weight. So, it is fortunate for the sweet-toothed slimmer that there is a wide variety of sugar substitutes available which can be used to give the sensation of sweetness but do not have the fattening power of real sugar. All the artificial sweeteners now sold are based on the sweetener saccharin which was first discovered as long ago as 1879. It has no food value itself but is 550 times as sweet as sugar. Sugar substitutes which are in tablet and liquid form are pure saccharin. The granular or powder substitutes contain saccharin coated granules of either sugar, lactose or sorbitol.

You can buy the following sugar substitutes at Boots:

	Contain	Sweetening power
Sweetex tablets	Saccharin	1 tablet=approx. 1 teaspoon sugar
Saccharin tablets BPC	Saccharin	1 tablet=approx. 1 teaspoon sugar
Sweetex liquid	Saccharin	1 drop=approx. $\frac{1}{4}$ teaspoon sugar
Sweetex powder	Sorbitol and saccharin	$\frac{1}{4}$ teaspoon=approx. 1 teaspoon sugar

Whichever form of sugar substitute you choose, you are bound to save yourself quite a number of calories. If you are used to drinking five cups of tea or coffee a day and putting two teaspoonsful of sugar into each, you could save about 350 Calories a day by using a sugar substitute. This could mean the loss of four pounds in a month just by cutting out sugar.

Soft Drinks

Water contains no calories or carbohydrates at all and must therefore qualify as the most slimming drink of all. But, although water is good for relieving thirst, it is not always what you want. If you like your tea and coffee black and sugarless, you can have as much of these as you like. If you cannot drink tea or coffee without milk, you will have to count the milk as part of your daily allowance. Of course, you can cut the calories by half if you use separated or low fat, powdered milk.

If you are in the habit of having a milky drink at night, try to reduce the calories by using either separated or powdered milk or by using half milk and half water.

Hot savoury drinks, made from Bovril, Marmite, Oxo, etc. can be very nourishing as well as warming, particularly in winter. These are all very low in calories – and keep you feeling full.

You can now get low calorie versions of most soft drinks, e.g. bitter lemon, fruit cordials, dry ginger, tonic water. Boots produce low calorie orange and lemon drinks and a lime juice cordial. These are all sweetened with saccharin instead of sugar and are virtually calorie free. (Warning: don't buy drinks sold for diabetics. These are sweetened with sorbitol which is just as fattening as sugar.) If you do not like the slightly bitter taste of saccharin, cordials are your best bet if you want a long drink and fruit juices, particularly tomato, if you want a shorter one.

Alcoholic Drinks

There are two factors which determine the fattening power of alcoholic drinks. One is the alcoholic content (a gramme of alcohol produces 7 Calories) and the other is the sugar content (a gramme of sugar produces 4 Calories). So, the drinks with the highest per cent proof and greatest sugar content will be the most damaging to your waistline. However, you have also got to take into account the amount that you drink. You will need to have a treble whisky to equal the calories in a pint of bitter. Drinking is such a personal matter, that it is difficult to lay down any hard and fast rules about the drinks you should have. The best thing you can do is to study the table on page 33 and decide for yourself how you can cut down – either by changing what you drink or how much you drink.

Carbohydrate cutters will have to show more restraint for alcoholic drinks than calorie cutters. A pint of stout would just about use up their total daily allowance. The same sort of rules apply: drink dry wine, dry vermouth or spirits if you can. If you must have the odd pint, make sure that the occasions are few and far between.

CHAPTER SEVEN

Cooking Methods for Slimmers

THE REASON for including a section about general cooking methods is that this is often where many slimmers go wrong. They buy all the right foods, but because they do not want to follow specific recipes all the time (and who does?), they carry on using their non-slimming basic cookery methods. One of the best examples of a food where the cooking method can drastically alter the calorie value is the mushroom. When you fry mushrooms, the calorie value jumps from 2 to 62 an ounce. So for 100 Calories, you can have over 3 lb. of raw mushrooms (or mushrooms cooked without fat) but less than 2 oz. of fried ones. (So, next time try poaching them gently in a little lemon juice.)

Although the next few paragraphs mainly explain how to cut calories during cooking, the same general methods apply to your cooking if you are a carbohydrate cutter.

Frying

Let us begin with frying just in case you were about to throw your frying pan out of the window after all that has been said about avoiding fats wherever possible. In one dictionary I looked at, the verb 'to fry' was given two meanings : to cook in fat and to cook in a frying pan. The first meaning should be pushed to the back of your mind — but there is no harm at all in using your frying pan without added fat. Actually, the strict cooking term 'frying' means driving off water from a food and you can do this as well in a frying pan as anywhere. Most frying pans sold today have a non-stick lining and one of these is a must if you want to fry with a minimum amount of fat. You can then use your frying pan for browning meat before casseroling it or for cooking some meat (like mince) completely. If the minced meat is put into the pan first and kept on the move, you will find that fat will soon melt from the meat. After about fifteen minutes, you can pour away all the excess fat and then add a small amount of thin stock to keep the meat moist. In this way, the fat in the meat has been *reduced,* not increased. Bacon addicts will also find that it is not necessary to add fat for frying. When the bacon has cooked, lift it out of the pan and blot it on absorbent kitchen paper to take away any surplus fat. If the bacon had a large strip of fat on it to begin with, you can remove all the visible fat with knife or scissors at this stage.

Another useful kitchen device for the slimmer who must fry is the griddle. This is particularly useful for frying foods, like thin steaks, which do not need much fat but do not make much either. You can brush the griddle with a little oil and this is all that will be needed to cook your steak.

Grilling

It is strange how 'grilling' is the 'good' word and 'frying' the 'bad' word in the slimmer's mind. If your normal method of grilling a steak or chop is to add a fair sized knob of butter to it before you stick it under the grill, then you might just as well fry it. Grilling is the usual method for cooking the thinner cuts of meat or fish, which are always comparatively tender. Provided you do not grill them too fiercely (either remove the grid from the pan or turn the grill down to medium heat after the first five minutes), you can grill steak or fish with a minimum of fat. The best way to apply a small amount of fat is to brush the food evenly with a little cooking oil. Foods like chops and sausages which make their own fat on heating are best placed on the grid so that the fat can drop underneath into the pan. It is best to cut off the visible fat from chops *after* cooking. You get more flavour this way. As before, always blot the grilled food with absorbent paper before serving to get rid of those surplus greasy calories which are not very pleasant to eat anyway.

The opportunity of flavouring your grilled foods should not be missed. Rub herbs and seasonings into the meat or fish before grilling them and you will be surprised how tasty the end result will be (see suggestions in 'Recipe Section', page 139).

Roasting and Baking

The only time true roasting can be seen these days is when an ox or pig is roasted on top of an open fire at a barbecue. Cooking in a closed oven is, strictly speaking, baking.

In recent years, baking has become a slimmer's cooking method, mainly due to the use of aluminium foil and high temperature resistant roasting bags and paper. Most types of meat and fish can be cooked very successfully without added fat if they are wrapped in foil or a roasting bag and baked in the oven. Not only does the foil or bag keep the food moist but it keeps in the natural flavour and any other flavours that you might like to add. (It keeps your oven beautifully clean too.)

This is often a wonderful way of cooking if you are cooking for yourself. If you choose vegetables that do not need a lot of cooking, you can put them on top of your meat or fish, wrap up the whole lot in foil and cook them together. Tomatoes, mushrooms, celery, sweetcorn and most frozen vegetables would all be suitable for this method. At the end of the baking time any fat that has come out of the meat will have collected in the foil or bag. Pour this away carefully and blot the excess fat off the outside of the meat. Do not be tempted to use this fatty juice for gravy unless you pour it into a bowl and let it settle so that the fat rises to the top. Then the bottom layer of non-fat meat juices can be reheated for the gravy.

You can bake vegetables, too, of course. Apart from the more common baked potatoes, why not try baked cabbage, marrow and parsnips, etc.?

Boiling, Stewing and Poaching

All these methods involve putting the food into liquid and cooking at boiling point or just under. Poaching is the term used for short cooking times. Boiling in meat cookery usually refers to larger pieces of meat; stewing to smaller pieces of meat. For the slimmer, they are all ideal cooking methods because none of them involve adding fat. The liquid you use can be water, flavoured with Oxo, Bovril, Marmite, etc. and herbs to taste — or you can use wine, beer or cider for more exotic meat dishes and vinegar for fish.

You can either stew meat in a covered pan on top of the cooker or it can be put in a casserole and cooked in the oven.

Boiling, of course, is the usual method for cooking vegetables. It is best to add your vegetables to about half an inch of salted boiling water and cook them in a covered pan for the shortest possible time to make them tender enough for eating. If you generally add a knob of butter to strained vegetables, either use a small knob of the low-fat spread 'Outline' (only half the calories of butter) or cook the vegetables with fresh herbs to add flavour.

Steaming

There is a widespread belief that if you steam fish you retain the maximum amount of nutritional goodness. In fact, this is untrue — grilling and baking are just as good, if not better.

Steaming is, however, a very good method for cooking vegetables because they shrink much less than meat and fish.

Pressure Cooking

Cooking under high pressure is a very good method for boiling or steaming all types of food in about one third of the time that it would take at atmospheric pressure.

CHAPTER EIGHT

Recipe Section

THE RECIPES are arranged as follows:

As far as possible, simple basic recipes which show you how to cook reasonably well known dishes in the least fattening way have been chosen. The calorie and CH Unit values of all the ingredients in the dishes are given so that you can see for yourself how the final figure for calories or CH Units per portion is arrived at. In most cases quantities given are for two people. For dishes that will keep perfectly well or which are not worth making up in small amounts, (e.g. salads), quantities required for four people are given.

I have also included several variations on the basic recipe where possible and have indicated the final calorie and CH Unit value for one portion.

You will find a list of recipes classified according to calorie and carbohydrate content at the back of the book (see Appendixes A and B).

45

Meat, Poultry and Offal Dishes

In the chapter on 'Cooking Methods for Slimmers' most of the more conventional methods for cooking meats were discussed. These can be summarised as follows:

- *If you ever fry meat, use as little fat as possible.*
- *Use roasting bags or tin foil when you are baking meat in an oven so that you do not have to baste with fat.*
- *Lightly brush meat with oil rather than adding a knob of fat when you are grilling.*
- *Do not add extra fat when you are cooking meats that make their own fat anyway. Cook gently to release a little fat and then continue to cook in this.*

The recipes in this section are based on these tips. They are *not* intended to add a unique experience in taste of the Cordon Bleu calibre, but rather to show how you can prepare good satisfying meals which are not necessarily too fattening.

Right: sweet and sour pork

46

Meat Dishes

(Calorie values are given for the very leanest of meat in all cases – beef and lamb, 75 Calories per ounce, veal and pork, 35 Calories per ounce. Adjust calorie values accordingly if you know your meat is slightly fatty.)

Basic Meat Casserole (for 2)

		Calories	CH units
½ oz.	*Butter or margarine*	115	0
8 oz.	*Stewing beef or lamb cut into chunks*	600	0
2	*Medium onions, sliced*	30	1½
	Stock cube (beef stock for lamb or beef)	15	½
½ pint	*Water*	0	0
½ lb.	*Carrots, sliced*	40	2
	Seasoning	0	0
		800	4

1. Melt fat in pan and brown meat evenly.
2. Transfer meat to ovenproof dish, leaving behind any surplus fat.
3. Soften onions in remaining fat. Add to meat.
4. Make up stock with cube and water. Add to meat and onions with carrots.
5. Cook in a cool oven (Gas Mark 3, 325°F., 163°C.) for 2–2½ hours until meat is tender.

CALORIES PER PORTION: 400
CH UNITS PER PORTION: 2

Sweet and Sour Pork

1. Follow recipe for Basic Meat Casserole, using lean pork fillet or belly of pork cut in cubes.
2. Omit carrots from basic recipe and add 2 oz. pineapple chunks (drained from syrup) plus ½ tablespoon soy sauce to the stock.
3. Slice a small red pepper (2 oz.) into rings and add ½ hour before serving.

CALORIES PER PORTION: 250
CH UNITS PER PORTION: 2

Pork with Apple and Cider

1. Follow recipe for Basic Meat Casserole, using pork fillet or belly of pork cut into cubes.
2. Omit carrots and onions from basic recipe and use ½ pint bottled cider instead of water for the stock.
3. Peel and cut a large cooking apple (about ½ lb.) into slices and add to the stock before cooking.

CALORIES PER PORTION: 295
CH UNITS PER PORTION: 5

Slimmers' Goulash

1. Follow recipe for Basic Meat Casserole, using 8 oz. stewing beef or veal.
2. Add 2 tablespoons paprika powder to pan when browning meat and make certain that meat is well covered.
3. Omit carrots from basic recipe and use 8 oz. canned tomatoes instead.
4. Drain the tomatoes and use the juice for the stock instead of water. Add the tomatoes ¼ hour before removing from oven.

CALORIES PER PORTION: 400 (beef), 240 (veal)
CH UNITS PER PORTION: 2 (beef and veal)

Curried Beef Casserole

1. Follow recipe for Basic Meat Casserole, using 8 oz. stewing or chuck beef.
2. Add one tablespoon curry powder when browning the meat.

CALORIES PER PORTION: 400
CH UNITS PER PORTION: 2

Lamb and Kidney Casserole

1. Follow recipe for Basic Meat Casserole, using 6 oz. stewing lamb, cut into cubes, and 2 oz. diced lamb's kidney.
2. Add a few sprigs of fresh mint to the casserole before putting in the oven. Otherwise add ½ teaspoon dried mint or rosemary.

CALORIES PER PORTION: 355
CH UNITS PER PORTION: 2

Lamb Stew

1. Follow recipe for Basic Meat Casserole, using 8 oz. stewing lamb, cut into cubes.
2. Cut a potato weighing about 4 oz. into cubes and add this with the carrots.

CALORIES PER PORTION: 450
CH UNITS PER PORTION: 4

Slimmers' Savoury Mince (for 2)

		Calories	CH units
6 oz.	*Minced beef*	450	0
2 oz.	*Liver, chopped*	80	0
2	*Medium onions, chopped*	30	$1\frac{1}{2}$
4 oz.	*Mushrooms, chopped*	8	0
2 tablespoons	*Tomato purée*	20	1
$\frac{1}{2}$ pint	*Water*	0	0
1	*Beef stock cube*	15	$\frac{1}{2}$
$\frac{1}{2}$ teaspoon	*Mixed herbs*	0	0
	Seasoning	0	0
		603	3

1. Wash minced beef and liver and put into a large saucepan or frying pan.
2. Cook gently at first so that some fat is released from the beef. Then turn heat up and brown the meat in its own fat. Pour off excess fat.
3. Remove meat and keep warm. Add chopped onions and mushrooms and cook in fat. Pour away any excess fat.
4. Return meat to pan. Add tomato purée, stock, herbs and seasoning. Cover and continue cooking over low heat for about $\frac{3}{4}$ hour or until meat is thoroughly cooked.

CALORIES PER PORTION: 300
CH UNITS PER PORTION: $1\frac{1}{2}$

Bolognese

1. If you have some calories or CH Units to spare you can make the Savoury Mince of a slightly thinner consistency by using $\frac{3}{4}$ pint water, or adding a can of tomatoes, and use it as a sauce for spaghetti, noodles or lasagne.
2. Allow 1 oz. raw pasta per portion (for slimmers) and cook in boiling salted water.
3. Drain and pour sauce over pasta.

CALORIES PER PORTION: 400
CH UNITS PER PORTION: 6

Veal Fricassée (for 2)

		Calories	CH units
8 oz.	Stewing veal or pie veal	280	0
2	Large onions	50	$2\frac{1}{2}$
$\frac{1}{2}$ lb.	Carrots	40	2
$\frac{1}{2}$ lb.	Celery, sliced	24	0
	Bay leaf	0	0
	Stock cube	15	$\frac{1}{2}$
$\frac{1}{4}$ pint	Water	0	0
$\frac{1}{4}$ pint	Milk (separated or made from low-fat skimmed powder)	45	$1\frac{1}{4}$
$\frac{1}{2}$ oz.	Fat	115	0
$\frac{1}{2}$ oz.	Flour	50	$2\frac{1}{2}$
		619	$8\frac{3}{4}$

1. Put meat and water to cover into saucepan and bring to boil. Discard water plus scum.
2. Add vegetables, bay leaf, stock cube and $\frac{1}{4}$ pint water to pan. Boil and simmer for about $\frac{3}{4}$ hour or until veal is tender.
3. Put veal and vegetables in warm dish, reserving stock. Make stock up to half a pint using low calorie milk.
4. Melt fat in pan, add flour and cook roux for a few minutes but do not allow to brown. Gradually add stock, continually stirring to form white sauce.
5. When sauce has thickened, pour over the meat and vegetables in ovenproof dish and reheat in oven at Gas Mark 4, 350°F., 177°C. for about $\frac{1}{2}$ hour.

CALORIES PER PORTION: 310
CH UNITS PER PORTION: $4\frac{1}{2}$

Left: veal fricassée

Grilling Recipes

In Chapter 7 it was suggested that you can best grill steak and chops by brushing them with oil before cooking. (If you prick sausages before cooking they will cook in their own fat.) In this way you use a minimum amount of fat. It was also suggested that you could add extra flavour to your grilled meat by rubbing various flavourings into the raw meat. The following table suggests which flavourings and garnishes are suited to which meats and gives you calorie values for the meats grilled in this way (assuming $\frac{1}{8}$ oz. oil is used per portion). All the dishes are carbohydrate-free.

		Calories	Flavouring	Garnish
Beef steak	4 oz.	300	Crushed garlic	Watercress
			Black peppercorns	Tomatoes
			Worcester sauce	
			Horseradish sauce	
			English mustard	
Gammon steak	4 oz.	360	German or French mustard	Pineapple
Lamb chop, all lean	4 oz.	300	Curry powder	Mint
Lamb chop, equal lean and fat	4 oz.	600	Grated cheese	Mushrooms
			Chopped tarragon	Parsley
Pork chop, all lean	4 oz.	140		Watercress
			Soy sauce	Tomatoes
Pork chop, equal lean and fat	4 oz.	520	German mustard	Poached apple rings
Veal fillet, all lean	4 oz.	140	Chopped parsley	Lemon
			Chives	
Sausage, beef or pork	4 oz.	400		

Slimmers' Kebabs

Kebabs are an excellent dish to prepare quickly when you have lots of leftovers to use up. The following are suitable for grilling:

Small cubes of liver
Small cubes of kidney
Small cubes of beef, lamb, pork or veal
Small onions
Half tomatoes
Half chipolata sausages
Button mushrooms
Small pieces of lean bacon, rolled up
Small pieces of green or red pepper
Small cubes of fresh pineapple.

1. Thread each skewer or kebab stick with alternate pieces of meat, offal, bacon or sausage and vegetable.
2. Season with salt and pepper, curry powder, ground ginger, etc.
3. Brush the meat and vegetables very lightly with oil.
4. Heat under a hot grill, turning as often as possible, for 10–15 minutes or until the ingredients are fully cooked.

● *Calories and CH Units for this dish depend on ingredients used. Refer to tables on pages 26–33.*

● *See illustration overleaf.*

Lamb Kebabs (for 2)

		Calories	CH units
8 oz.	*Marinaded stewing lamb (see page 55) cut into cubes*	600	0
8	*Small onions or shallots*	80	4
8	*Button mushrooms*	8	0
8	*Small tomatoes*	40	$1\frac{1}{4}$
8	*Bay leaves*	0	0
	Small amount of oil for initial brushing	55	0
		783	$5\frac{1}{4}$

1. Thread each kebab stick with alternate pieces of lamb, onion, mushroom, tomato and bay leaf. (Use fresh bay leaves if available, otherwise soak dried ones for 5 minutes.)
2. Brush lightly with oil and grill under a preheated grill on medium heat for 20 minutes, turning often.

CALORIES PER PORTION: 390
CH UNITS PER PORTION: $2\frac{3}{4}$

Marinading

Another cooking technique which you can use to both tenderise and add extra flavour to your grilled meat is *marinading* (i.e. soaking it in a basic mixture of oil, vinegar and seasoning). Prepare the marinade, pour it over the raw, washed meat and leave it in the fridge (or a cold larder) for a minimum of 2 hours for cubed meat or overnight for larger joints.

Meat	Suggested marinade
Beef	*6 tablespoons oil* *½ pint beer* *1 clove of garlic, crushed* *2 tablespoons lemon juice* *1 level tablespoon castor sugar* *Seasoning*
Chicken	*6 tablespoons dry white wine or cider* *3 tablespoons oil* *1 small onion, finely chopped* *1 teaspoon mixed herbs* *Seasoning*
Lamb (i)	*2 tablespoons lemon juice* *3 tablespoons oil* *Seasoning (e.g. crushed bay leaf and allspice,*
Lamb (ii)	*¼ pint vinegar* *2 tablespoons oil* *1 onion, sliced* *2 bay leaves* *Seasoning*
Pork	*1 small onion, finely grated* *¼ level teaspoon dry mustard* *1 tablespoon Worcester sauce* *3 tablespoons lemon juice* *Seasoning (use small amount cayenne pepper)*

When you remove your meat from the marinade blot it dry and then grill normally.

Left: kebabs

Roasting and Baking

In Chapter 7, I mentioned how useful aluminium foil and roasting bags are for slimmers because they enable you to cook meat in its own juices without adding any extra fat. The following recipes illustrate this point.

Roast Joint and Baked Vegetables (Basic Recipe)

1. Rub salt into the joint and put it in a roasting bag. Loosely seal the bag and place in a roasting tin. Make several small slits in the top of the bag with a sharp knife or scissors.
2. Cook at Gas Mark 6, 400°F., 204°C. (20–30 minutes per lb. for

Meat	Suitable joint for roasting	Allow per person
Beef	Sirloin, topside, rump, all rib cuts, fillet, brisket	$\frac{1}{2}-\frac{3}{4}$ lb. with bone 4–6 oz. without bone
Chicken, Turkey or Duck	Whole bird, stuffed (for stuffings, see page 72)	$\frac{1}{2}$ lb. with bone
Lamb or Mutton	Leg, shoulder, loin, best end of neck or stuffed, boned breast (for stuffings, see page 72)	$\frac{1}{2}-\frac{3}{4}$ lb. with bone 4–6 oz. without bone
Pork	Hand and spring, blade, loin, leg or spare rib	$\frac{1}{2}-\frac{3}{4}$ lb. with bone 4–6 oz. without bone
Veal	Loin, leg, boned shoulder, stuffed breast (for stuffings, see page 72)	$\frac{1}{2}-\frac{3}{4}$ lb. with bone 4–6 oz. without bone

beef, 25–30 minutes per lb. for all other meats) or follow directions given with bag.

3. Half an hour before the joint is done, open the bag and put in the prepared vegetables. Reseal bag and continue cooking.

4. Slit bag and pour fatty juices into a basin or jug. Keep meat warm. When the fat has risen to the top of the juices, pour this off so that you are just left with the non-fatty meat juices. Reheat these, with a stock cube for extra flavour if wanted, and serve with the meat as a thin gravy.

The following table shows you the cuts of each type of meat that are suitable for roasting, suitable vegetables for an accompaniment and the calorie value per portion for the meat.

Suitable vegetables for baking	Flavourings (rub over skin or insert between skin and flesh)	Approx. calories per portion (assuming this is 4 oz. lean meat only)
Whole onions, parboiled potatoes, half parsnips, pieces of marrow, carrots	Mustard, yeast extract, ground black peppercorns, chopped chives	30
Potatoes, onions, chipolata sausages, oranges, cherries	Paprika, chopped rosemary, oregano, lemon peel (or put large cooking apple inside bird)	140 (chicken and turkey) 280 (duck)
Parboiled potatoes, turnips, swedes, onions	Chopped garlic, chopped rosemary, chopped mint	300
Apples cut into quarters, parboiled potatoes, onions, tomatoes	Dried sage, chopped onion, mustard, curry powder	140
Parboiled potatoes, quartered carrots, quartered onions	Chopped garlic, rosemary, thyme, zest of lemon	140

Left: roast pork; leave the crackling for the slimmer members of the family.
Above: Mexican chicken

Poultry Dishes

Basic Chicken Casserole (for 2)

			Calories	CH units
1 oz.		Butter	225	0
2	Chicken pieces about 6 oz. each		420	0
1		Onion, sliced	15	$\frac{3}{4}$
1		Clove garlic, crushed	2	0
		Pinch mixed herbs	0	0
1		Chicken stock cube	15	$\frac{1}{2}$
$\frac{3}{4}$ pint		Water	0	0
4 oz.		Mushrooms, sliced	8	0
		Seasoning	0	0
			685	$1\frac{1}{4}$

1. Melt butter in frying pan and brown chicken pieces evenly.
2. Transfer chicken to ovenproof dish.
3. Fry onion and garlic in remaining fat.
4. Add onion, garlic and herbs to the chicken.
5. Make up the chicken stock using cube and water. Pour over rest of ingredients. Season to taste.
6. Cover dish and cook in a moderate oven (Gas Mark 4, 350°F., 177°C.) for 1¼ hours. Add mushrooms and continue cooking for another ¼ hour.

CALORIES PER PORTION: 345
CH UNITS PER PORTION: ¾

Mexican Chicken

1. Follow recipe for Basic Chicken Casserole.
2. Add rings of sliced red pepper (about 2 oz.) and ¼ teaspoon chilli powder to the ingredients before cooking.

CALORIES PER PORTION: 355
CH UNITS PER PORTION: ¾

● See illustration on previous page.

Chicken and Tomato Casserole

1. Follow recipe for Basic Chicken Casserole.
2. Dissolve the chicken stock cube in a little tomato juice from a can of tomatoes. Add this, plus the rest of the tomatoes and juice, to the chicken.

CALORIES PER PORTION: 360
CH UNITS PER PORTION: 1½

Duck à l'Orange

1. Follow recipe for Basic Chicken Casserole, using two 4-oz. duck pieces, but omit the stock and the mushrooms.
2. Add $\frac{3}{4}$ pint unsweetened orange juice to duck instead of the chicken stock.
3. Before serving, garnish duck with sections from a fresh orange.

CALORIES PER PORTION: 445
CH UNITS PER PORTION: 5

Coq au Vin

1. Follow recipe for Basic Chicken Casserole, but omit the chicken stock and mixed herbs.
2. Add $\frac{1}{2}$ pint dry red wine instead of the chicken stock and use a bay leaf instead of mixed herbs.
3. Cook as in basic recipe.

CALORIES PER PORTION: 425
CH UNITS PER PORTION: $5\frac{1}{2}$

Chicken Curry

1. Follow recipe for Basic Chicken Casserole.
2. Add 2 teaspoons curry powder to the butter used for frying and coat chicken pieces in it.

CALORIES PER PORTION: 345
CH UNITS PER PORTION: $\frac{3}{4}$

Offal Dishes

Because of its low fat and high protein content, offal is less fattening than beef lamb and pork. The two main methods of cooking offal are grilling and braising or casseroling. Here are a few basic recipes:

Grilled Liver (for 2)

		Calories	CH units
8 oz.	*Liver*	320	0
	Cold milk	0	0
	Little oil	25	0
		345	0

1. Cut liver into pieces not thicker than $\frac{1}{2}$ inch.
2. Put into a shallow dish and cover with milk. Leave for at least $\frac{1}{2}$ hour. Drain and blot dry with kitchen paper.
3. Brush pieces on both sides with a very small amount of oil.
4. Cook liver under a very hot grill for a few minutes on each side. (It is cooked when small beads of blood appear on the surface.)

CALORIES PER PORTION: 170
CH UNITS PER PORTION: 0

Liver Parcels (for 2)

		Calories	CH units
8 oz.	*Liver*	320	0
2	*Lean bacon rashers*	115	0
1	*Small onion*	10	$\frac{1}{2}$
2 oz.	*Mushrooms*	4	0
2 medium	*Tomatoes*	20	1
4 oz.	*Frozen peas*	80	2
	Worcester sauce to taste	0	0
	Salt and pepper	0	0
		549	$3\frac{1}{2}$

1. Place the liver on a large piece of aluminium foil.
2. Chop the bacon and onion, slice the mushrooms and tomatoes.
3. Layer the bacon, onion, mushrooms and tomatoes on the liver, season with Worcester sauce and salt and pepper.
4. Place frozen peas on top.
5. Carefully seal the foil into a parcel and place on a baking dish.
6. Cook for 35 minutes (Gas Mark 4, 350°F., 177°C.).

CALORIES PER PORTION: 275
CH UNITS PER PORTION: $1\frac{3}{4}$

Kidneys in oxtail sauce

Liver Casserole (for 2)

		Calories	CH units
8 oz.	*Liver*	320	0
2	*Large onions*	50	$2\frac{1}{2}$
3 (*about 6 oz.*)	*Sticks celery, chopped*	18	0
Tin (*about 8 oz.*)	*Tomatoes*	40	2
	Pinch mixed herbs	0	0
	Seasoning	0	0
		428	$4\frac{1}{2}$

1. Cut the liver into serving sized pieces and place in a casserole dish.
2. Peel and slice the onions into rings and lay on top of the liver together with the chopped celery.
3. Empty the tin of tomatoes into the casserole dish. Add the seasoning and mixed herbs. Cover and cook for $2-2\frac{1}{2}$ hours in a cool oven (Gas Mark 2, 300°F., 149°C.).

CALORIES PER PORTION: 215
CH UNITS PER PORTION: $2\frac{1}{4}$

Kidneys in Oxtail Sauce (for 2)

		Calories	CH units
½ oz.	*Margarine*	115	0
8 oz.	*Kidneys*	240	0
2	*Large onions*	50	2½
½ packet	*Oxtail soup powder*	100	3
¼ pint	*Water*	0	0
	Seasoning	0	0
	Chopped parsley	0	0
		505	5½

1. Melt the fat in a frying pan or large saucepan.
2. Cut the kidneys into bite sized pieces (lambs' kidneys are smaller and can simply be cut into two). Chop onions finely.
3. Toss the kidneys very quickly in the melted fat. Add onions.
4. ᐧDissolve the soup powder in the cold water. Add to the pan, bring to the boil stirring continuously. Add seasoning to taste.
5. When sauce has thickened, reduce heat to a simmer, cover pan and continue cooking for a further 15 minutes.
6. Add the chopped parsley just before serving.

CALORIES PER PORTION: 250
CH UNITS PER PORTION: 2¾

● *See illustration on previous page.*

Oxtail Stew (for 2)

		Calories	CH units
½ oz.	*Lard*	130	0
1 lb.	*Oxtail joints*	640	0
1	*Large onion*	25	1¼
1 (4 oz.)	*Large carrot*	20	1
1 (2 oz.)	*Stick celery*	6	0
1 (2 oz.)	*Small turnip*	10	½
1	*Beef stock cube*	15	½
1 pint	*Water*	0	0
1	*Bay leaf*	0	0
6	*Peppercorns*	0	0
	Salt	0	0
		846	3¼

1. Remove all visible fat from joints.
2. Melt fat in saucepan. Brown meat quickly.
3. Remove meat and add chopped vegetables to remaining fat. Fry quickly.
4. Make up stock with cube and water. Add gradually to pan.
5. Return meat to pan and add bay leaf and seasoning to taste.
6. Bring stock to boil, reduce heat to a simmer and cook for 3 hours or until the meat is tender.

CALORIES PER PORTION: 425
CH UNITS PER PORTION: 1¾

Tripe and Onions (for 2)

		Calories	CH units
1 lb.	Dressed tripe	480	0
2	Large onions	50	$2\frac{1}{2}$
$\frac{1}{2}$ pint	Low calorie milk	95	$2\frac{3}{4}$
	Pinch ground mace	0	0
$\frac{1}{2}$ tablespoon	Cornflour	50	$2\frac{1}{2}$
	Salt and pepper	0	0
		675	$7\frac{3}{4}$

1. Wash tripe and cut into 2-inch squares.
2. Slice onions finely.
3. Put tripe and onions in saucepan together with milk and mace. (Reserve 2 tablespoons of cold milk.)
4. Bring to boil, reduce heat to simmer and continue cooking until tripe is tender (about $\frac{3}{4}$ hour).
5. Mix cornflour to smooth paste with rest of milk. Add to pan. Continue cooking until sauce thickens. Season to taste.

CALORIES PER PORTION: 335
CH UNITS PER PORTION: 4

MOIRA SHIPPARD

Polish Slimmers' Tripe (for 2)

		Calories	CH units
2 (say 8 oz.)	Leeks	80	2
4 (say 4 oz.)	Carrots	80	.4
2 (4 oz.)	Sticks celery	12	.0
1 lb.	Dressed tripe	480	0
1	Large onion	25	$1\frac{1}{4}$
$\frac{1}{2}$ oz.	Butter	115	0
1	Chicken stock cube	15	$\frac{1}{2}$
$\frac{1}{4}$ pint	Water	0	0
	Salt and pepper	0	0
		807	$7\frac{3}{4}$

To serve as garnish:
Ground ginger
Paprika
Marjoram
Parmesan cheese (1 teaspoon per person)

1. Prepare vegetables and cut into small pieces.
2. Wash tripe and cut into narrow strips.
3. Slice onion and fry in butter until soft.
4. Dissolve the stock cube in the water and add to the onion.
5. Add the tripe and onion to the pan and simmer gently for 30–40 minutes until the vegetables are soft.
6. Serve in soup bowls garnished with a pinch of ground ginger, paprika, marjoram and Parmesan cheese or, alternatively, serve the garnish separately.

N.B. Use only the correct amount of water since tripe gives off a lot of water. Before serving you can strain off any unnecessary liquid.

CALORIES PER PORTION: 400
CH UNITS PER PORTION: 4

Cooked Meat Dishes

These have been included in this section as when slimming you will often find that your food bill costs more than before, even though you are eating less. It is unfortunate that the bulky carbohydrate foods such as flour, sugar and bread are comparatively cheaper and when you start replacing these by more fresh meat and vegetables you are almost bound to notice the difference in cost. So, in these circumstances, it is more important than ever to be able to devise dishes which you can make with the leftovers from a joint – dishes, in fact, which are low in calories and carbohydrates. Five basic recipes are given – for a meat loaf, meatburgers, a risotto, a cottage pie and a mould. You can follow the same basic methods using any cold minced meat. The chart at the end of each basic recipe gives you the comparative calorie and carbohydrate values.

Basic Meat Loaf (for 4)

		Calories	CH units
1 lb.	*Cooked minced beef*	1,200	0
2	*Hardboiled eggs, finely chopped*	180	0
1	*Large onion, finely chopped*	25	$1\frac{1}{4}$
	Pinch mixed herbs	0	0
	Seasoning	0	0
1	*Egg*	90	0
		1,495	$1\frac{1}{4}$

1. Mix together meat, chopped hardboiled eggs, onion, herbs and seasoning.
2. Bind all ingredients together using raw egg.
3. Place in a loaf tin, covering top with greaseproof paper, or shape into a loaf and wrap in tinfoil.
4. Cook in fairly hot oven (Gas Mark 5, 375°F., 190°C.) for about $\frac{3}{4}$ hour. Remove greaseproof paper or open up foil parcel for about 10 minutes to let the top brown.

Meat	Calories per portion	CH Units per portion
Minced, cooked beef	375	$\frac{1}{2}$
chicken	215	$\frac{1}{2}$
lamb	375	$\frac{1}{2}$
pork	215	$\frac{1}{2}$
veal	215	$\frac{1}{2}$

Basic Meatburgers (for 4)

Ingredients as for basic meat loaf plus oil.

1. After mixing all ingredients, shape mixture into eight flat cakes.
2. Brush the meatburgers very lightly with oil and grill under a hot grill for about 15 minutes, turning once.

Calorie and CH Unit values per portion as for basic meat loaf but add 10 calories per portion for oil.

Basic Risotto (for 4)

		Calories	CH units
1 pint	*Stock (make using beef or chicken stock cube depending on meat used)*	15	$\frac{1}{2}$
4 oz.	*Uncooked rice*	400	20
1 (4 oz.)	*Red or green pepper*	40	0
2 (3 oz.)	*Sticks celery*	12	0
8 oz.	*Minced cooked beef*	600	0
	Pinch dried herbs	0	0
	Seasoning	0	0
		1,067	$20\frac{1}{2}$

1. Boil the stock. Add the rice and cook until the rice is nearly tender.
2. Cut up the pepper and celery and add, together with cooked meat, to the rice.
3. Add dried herbs and season to taste.

Meat	Calories per portion	CH Units per portion
Minced, cooked beef	265	5
chicken	185	5
lamb	265	5
pork	185	5
veal	185	5

Basic Slimmers' Cottage Pie (for 4)

		Calories	CH units
1	Large onion	25	$1\frac{1}{4}$
1	Large carrot	20	1
$\frac{1}{2}$ oz.	Fat	115	0
1 lb.	Minced cooked beef	1,200	0
2	Egg yolks	150	0
$\frac{1}{4}$ pint	Stock	15	$\frac{1}{2}$
	Pinch mixed herbs	0	0
2	Egg whites	30	0
	Seasoning	0	0
$\frac{1}{2}$ oz.	Parmesan cheese	60	0
		1,615	$2\frac{3}{4}$

1. Chop onion and carrot finely.
2. Melt fat and fry meat, onion and carrot in it.
3. Separate the eggs and add the yolks plus stock and herbs to the meat and vegetables.
4. Mix well and cook for a few minutes. Transfer to ovenproof dish.
5. Whisk up egg whites till they are stiff. Add seasoning and spread meringue over meat mixture.
6. Sprinkle Parmesan cheese over top of meringue.
7. Cook in a fairly hot oven (Gas Mark 5, 375°F., 190°C.) for about 15 minutes or put under a hot grill until the meringue is golden brown.

Meat	Calories per portion	CH Units per portion
Minced, cooked beef	405	$\frac{3}{4}$
chicken	240	$\frac{3}{4}$
lamb	405	$\frac{3}{4}$
pork	240	$\frac{3}{4}$
veal	240	$\frac{3}{4}$

If you prefer a more conventional potato topping for your cottage pie, you can leave out the eggs and make the topping from 6 oz. cooked potatoes, mashed with 1 tablespoon milk.

CALORIES PER PORTION: as above
CH UNITS PER PORTION: $2\frac{1}{4}$

Basic Meat Mould (for 4)

		Calories	CH units
2 oz.	Cooked carrots, cubed	10	$\frac{1}{2}$
2 oz.	Cooked peas	40	1
$\frac{1}{2}$ oz.	Gelatine	50	0
1 pint	Stock	15	$\frac{1}{2}$
	Seasoning	0	0
1 lb.	Minced cooked beef (you can use a mixture of meats or meat plus offal)	1,200	0
		1,315	2

1. Put the cooked vegetables at the bottom of the mould.
2. Make up the gelatine by first dissolving the powder in a little cold stock and then adding the rest of the hot stock to this. Season.
3. Pour a little of this gelatine over the vegetables to cover them. Allow this to set.
4. Put meat into the mould and pour the rest of the gelatine over it. Allow to set.
5. To make it easier to turn out the mould, hold it briefly under a hot tap and let the water trickle down the sides of the mould.
6. Invert on to a previously wetted plate (wetting the plate makes it easier to slide the mould to a central position on the plate).

Meat	Calories per portion	CH Units per portion
Minced, cooked beef	330	$\frac{1}{2}$
chicken	165	$\frac{1}{2}$
lamb	330	$\frac{1}{2}$
pork	165	$\frac{1}{2}$
veal	165	$\frac{1}{2}$

Right: mushroom, tomato and celery stuffing

Stuffings

Stuffing (or forcemeat) is used in boned joints and birds for three reasons:

- to keep the bird or joint in shape
- to add flavour
- to make a small bird or joint go further.

There is no reason why you should deny yourself the pleasure of eating stuffing while you are slimming as long as you keep to a normal sized portion of any of the following stuffings. Cooking instructions are not given as the stuffing is cooked at the same time as bird or joint.

Packeted Stuffings (Sage and Onion, Parsley and Thyme, etc.)

Follow the directions on the packet — usually 1 tablespoon of stuffing and 2 tablespoons of water per portion.

CALORIES PER PORTION: 35
CH UNITS PER PORTION: $1\frac{1}{2}$

Mushroom, Tomato and Celery Stuffing (for 4)

		Calories	CH units
2 slices	White bread	160	7
$\frac{1}{2}$ lb.	Tomatoes	40	2
$\frac{1}{4}$ lb.	Mushrooms	8	0
6 (about $\frac{1}{2}$ lb.)	Sticks celery	24	0
2 tablespoons	Lemon juice	4	0
		236	9

1. Soak bread in water. Squeeze out excess water.
2. Skin tomatoes by placing them in boiling water for a minute or so. Chop them finely.
3. Wash and slice the mushrooms and celery. Poach for about 10 minutes in lemon juice.
4. Add the tomatoes and bread and continue cooking for 5 minutes.

CALORIES PER PORTION: 60
CH UNITS PER PORTION: $2\frac{1}{4}$

- See illustration on previous page.

Rice and Liver Stuffing (for 4)

		Calories	CH units
2 oz.	Chicken liver, chopped	80	0
½ oz.	Uncooked rice	50	2½
2 (4 oz.)	Small onions, chopped	20	1
2 tablespoons	Chopped parsley	0	0
½ teaspoon	Rosemary	0	0
	Salt and pepper	0	0
		150	3½

1. Cook the chicken liver and rice in 4 tablespoons of salted water until the rice is soft. Drain away excess water.
2. Add the chopped onion, parsley and rosemary, and season to taste.

CALORIES PER PORTION: 40
CH UNITS PER PORTION: 1

Corn and Onion Stuffing (for 4)

		Calories	CH units
3 slices	White bread	240	10½
Can (about 8 oz.)	Sweetcorn, drained	200	8
1 teaspoon	Grated onion	5	¼
	Salt and pepper	0	0
		445	18¾

1. Soak bread in water and squeeze out excess.
2. Add sweetcorn, onion and seasoning and mix all together.

CALORIES PER PORTION: 110
CH UNITS PER PORTION: 4¾

Lemon Stuffing (for 4)

		Calories	CH units
2 slices	White bread	160	7
2 oz.	Chicken, pigs' or calves' liver	80	0
	Rind of one lemon	0	0
	Half a medium cooking apple grated (optional)	20	1
2 teaspoons	Grated onion	10	½
	Salt and pepper	0	0
		270	8½

1. Soak bread in water, squeeze out excess water.
2. Chop liver finely.
3. Grate the lemon, apple and onion.
4. Mix all ingredients and season to taste.

N.B.   This stuffing is especially good with chicken or veal.

CALORIES PER PORTION: 65
CH UNITS PER PORTION: 2

Chestnut Stuffing (for 4)

		Calories	CH units
4 oz.	White bread	280	12
8 oz.	Unsweetened chestnut purée	400	16
1 tablespoon	Lemon juice	2	0
	Seasoning	0	0
1 tablespoon	Mixed herbs	0	0
1	Egg	90	0
		772	28

1. Soak the bread in water and then squeeze out excess moisture.
2. Mix the chestnut purée, lemon juice, seasoning and herbs with the bread and bind all ingredients with the beaten egg.

CALORIES PER PORTION: 195
CH UNITS PER PORTION: 7

Sausage and Celery Stuffing (for 4)

		Calories	CH units
3 (6 oz.)	Sticks celery	18	0
8 oz.	Sausage meat	800	8
1 tablespoon	Lemon juice	2	0
		820	8

1. Wash the celery and cut into small pieces about ½ inch long.
2. Mix celery pieces with sausage meat and lemon juice.

CALORIES PER PORTION: 205
CH UNITS PER PORTION: 2

Further ideas for ingredients to use in stuffings can be found in the section on 'Stuffed Vegetables' on page 116.

Fish Dishes

In the earlier section on cookery methods, it was stressed how useful fish could be to you as a slimmer as long as you forget all about deep fried fish in hot batter or breadcrumbs. The following recipes illustrate the methods which were suggested – poaching, grilling and baking. In general, white fish such as plaice, turbot, cod, haddock, halibut, etc. are best baked and served with a sauce or poached, whereas darker oily fish such as herrings and mackerel can be grilled or baked without a sauce.

Fish cutlets in a foil parcel

Baked Herrings with Vinegar Sauce (for 2)

		Calories	CH units
2	Herrings (about 4 oz. each)	520	0
4 tablespoons	Vinegar	2	0
Sauce			
$\frac{1}{4}$ pint	Vinegar	5	0
$\frac{1}{4}$ pint	Water	0	0
1 level teaspoon	Cornflour	30	$1\frac{1}{2}$
		557	$1\frac{1}{2}$

1. Place herrings in an ovenproof dish with vinegar. Bake (Gas Mark 4, 350°F., 177°C.) for about 30 minutes.
2. To make the sauce, mix the cornflour with a little of the liquid to form a smooth paste.
3. Boil rest of liquid and pour on to blended cornflour.
4. Return to pan and stir continuously until sauce has thickened.
5. Pour sauce over herrings just before serving.

CALORIES PER PORTION: 280
CH UNITS PER PORTION: $\frac{3}{4}$

Baked Fish with Egg Sauce (for 2)

		Calories	CH units
2	Pieces of cod or haddock (about 6 oz. each)	240	0
	Seasoning	0	0
1 level tablespoon	Cornflour	75	$3\frac{1}{2}$
$\frac{1}{2}$ pint	Milk made from low-fat powder	95	$2\frac{3}{4}$
2 tablespoons	Lemon juice	2	0
	Hardboiled egg, chopped	90	0
	Watercress for garnish	0	0
		502	$6\frac{1}{4}$

1. Sprinkle the seasoning on the cod and bake (Gas Mark 5, 375°F., 190°C.) in an ovenproof dish (or foil) for about 20 minutes.
2. Mix cornflour with a little milk to form a smooth paste.
3. Boil rest of milk and lemon juice; add to cornflour.
4. .Pour on to blended cornflour and return to pan. Cook until thickened, stirring continuously.
5. Add the chopped egg to the sauce and pour over fish before serving.
6. Garnish with watercress.

CALORIES PER PORTION: 250
CH UNITS PER PORTION: $3\frac{1}{4}$

Cheesey Baked Fish
Add 1 oz. grated cheese to the white sauce instead of the chopped egg and pour over fish. Just before serving, sprinkle another ounce of grated cheese over the top and brown under the grill for a few minutes.

CALORIES PER PORTION: 325
CH UNITS PER PORTION: $3\frac{1}{4}$

Fish Cutlets in a Foil Parcel (for 2)

		Calories	CH units
2 (12 oz.)	Cod or haddock cutlets or steaks	240	0
1 (about 4 oz.)	Green pepper cut into rings	40	0
2	Tomatoes, thinly sliced	20	1
4 oz.	Mushrooms, thinly sliced	8	0
4 oz.	Celery, sliced	12	0
2 tablespoons	Lemon juice	2	0
	Seasoning	0	0
		322	1

1. Wash the fish cutlets and place each on a piece of aluminium foil large enough to wrap around the fish.
2. Prepare the vegetables and gently poach them all together in the lemon juice for about 10 minutes.
3. Pile the mixed vegetables on to each of the fish steaks. Sprinkle with salt and pepper and the rest of the lemon juice.
4. Wrap up the foil parcels and put on a baking tray. Bake for about 30 minutes (Gas Mark 4, 350°F., 177°C.).

CALORIES PER PORTION: 160
CH UNITS PER PORTION: $\frac{1}{2}$

● See illustration on page 75.

Sweet and Sour Baked Fish

Brush both sides of the fish cutlets with soy sauce and then sprinkle with a little ginger. Add vegetables as before.

CALORIES AND CH UNITS PER PORTION AS ABOVE.

Fruity Baked Fish

Instead of vegetables, pile small pieces of two medium sized oranges on to the fish and sprinkle with lemon juice.

CALORIES PER PORTION: 160
CH UNITS PER PORTION: $2\frac{1}{2}$

Fish Fillets in a Foil Parcel (for 2)

		Calories	CH units
4 (about 12 oz.)	Small fillets of plaice, or any white fish	240	0
	Little oil (no more than a teaspoon)	25	0
4 oz.	Mushrooms, finely sliced	8	0
½	Cucumber, finely sliced	24	0
	Grated lemon rind	0	0
	Seasoning	0	0
	Juice of half lemon	5	0
		302	0

1. Brush the fillets very lightly with oil.
2. Prepare two pieces of foil large enough to wrap around the fillets. Put one fillet on each piece of foil, skin side down.
3. Place slices of mushroom and cucumber on to each fillet. Sprinkle with lemon rind, seasoning and lemon juice.
4. Place second fillet on top of first, skin side uppermost. Sprinkle with more seasoning and lemon juice.
5. Fold the foil to form two parcels and put these on a shallow baking tray. Bake for about 30 minutes (Gas Mark 4, 350°F., 177°C.).

CALORIES PER PORTION: 150
CH UNITS PER PORTION: 0

Fruity Fillets

Use $\frac{1}{2}$ lb. grapes, halved and pipped, instead of mushrooms and cucumber between the fillets.

CALORIES PER PORTION: 195
CH UNITS PER PORTION: 4

Baked Stuffed Fish (for 2)

		Calories	CH units
1 (about 1½ lb.)	Large haddock or plaice	480	0
Stuffing			
¼ lb.	Chopped mushrooms	8	0
1 medium	Tomato, skinned and sliced	10	1
2	Small onions, chopped	20	1
2 tablespoons	Soft breadcrumbs	70	3
1	Small clove of garlic, crushed	2	0
1	Egg	90	0
		680	5

Garnish
Lemon slices
Parsley

1. Prepare the fish ; remove scales, fins, tail and internal organs if this has not been done already. Wash the fish in cold water and then dry on a towel or kitchen paper.
2. Prepare the stuffing. Mix the mushrooms, tomato, onions, breadcrumbs and garlic and bind with the beaten egg.
3. Fill the cavity of the fish with the stuffing and secure with skewers or with needle and thread.
4. Put the fish in an ovenproof dish or wrap in foil and bake for 30 minutes (Gas Mark 4, 350°F., 177°C.).
5. Garnish with lemon slices and parsley.

CALORIES PER PORTION: 340
CH UNITS PER PORTION: 2½

N.B.   When preparing plaice for stuffing, make a slit down the centre bone on the white side and form a pocket for stuffing on either side of the slit by filleting the flesh from the bone.

Variations
Other stuffings suitable for fish will be found in the recipe section on stuffings, e.g. corn and onion stuffing on page 73, and in the section on 'Stuffed Vegetables' on page 116.

79

Left: fruity fillets

Grilled Herrings or Trout (for 2)

	Calories		CH units
2 *(about 12 oz.)* **Whole herrings or trout**	780 (herrings)	300 (trout)	0
Seasoning	0	0	0
	780	300	0

1. Cut 2 or 3 deep gashes in the sides of the fish to allow the heat to reach the centre.
2. Sprinkle seasoning on to the fish and cook steadily under the grill for about 5–8 minutes for each side.
3. Serve by itself with vegetables or with a suitable sauce, e.g. Pepper and Tomato Sauce, page 137.

CALORIES PER PORTION: 150 (trout), 390 (herrings)
CH UNITS PER PORTION: 0

● *See illustration on page 135.*

Variations

If you grill white fish you will probably need to add a little fat. The best way is to brush the fish with a very small amount of oil or melted fat. Small quantities of dried herbs can be rubbed into the fish to add extra flavour. Suitable herbs are marjoram, parsley and tarragon. White fish is best served with a flavoured white sauce, e.g.

Cucumber Sauce	page 136.
Tomato Sauce	page 136.
Parsley Sauce	page 136.
Seafood Sauce	page 136.

MOIRA SHIPPARD

Fish Casserole (for 2)

		Calories	CH units
12 oz.	Cod, haddock or plaice	240	0
8 oz. (can)	Tomatoes	40	2
4 oz.	Button mushrooms	8	0
1 teaspoon	Worcester sauce	0	0
	Seasoning	0	0
		288	2

1. Wash and flake the fish into an ovenproof dish.
2. Empty the whole can of tomatoes into the dish.
3. Add the washed mushrooms and Worcester sauce.
4. Season to taste and bake, covered, for about 30 minutes (Gas Mark 4, 350°F., 177°C.).

CALORIES PER PORTION: 145
CH UNITS PER PORTION: 1

Variations
Fish in Wine

Use $\frac{1}{4}$ pint of cheap, dry white wine and $\frac{1}{2}$ lb. skinned tomatoes instead of the tinned tomatoes.

CALORIES PER PORTION: 190
CH UNITS PER PORTION: $3\frac{1}{2}$

Fish in Cider

Use $\frac{1}{4}$ pint of dry cider and $\frac{1}{2}$ lb. skinned tomatoes instead of tinned tomatoes. Use onion rings cut from a small onion instead of mushrooms.

CALORIES PER PORTION: 170
CH UNITS PER PORTION: $2\frac{1}{2}$

(Herring and trout are also tasty when baked in cider.)

Poached Fish (for 2)

		Calories	CH units
4 (about 12 oz.)	*Small cutlets or fillets of white fish*	240	0
$\frac{1}{4}$ *pint*	*Chicken stock from stock cube*	15	$\frac{1}{2}$
		255	$\frac{1}{2}$

1. Place cutlets or fillets in a large saucepan or frying pan and just cover with stock.
2. Poach gently until the fish is just cooked, i.e. it will just flake away from the bone.

CALORIES PER PORTION: 125

CH UNITS PER PORTION: $\frac{1}{4}$

Variations

Instead of chicken stock, use $\frac{1}{4}$ pint of dry white wine or cider. You could flavour the stock with a few allspice or black peppercorns. The poached fish can either be served in the thin sauce in which it has cooked (170 Calories per portion, $2\frac{1}{2}$ CH Units for wine, and 150 Calories, $1\frac{1}{2}$ CH Units for cider) or the sauce can be thickened in the following way:

Keep a little of your chosen stock, add $\frac{1}{2}$ oz. cornflour to it and blend it to a smooth paste. When the fish is cooked, take it out of the pan and keep it hot. Add the blended cornflour, bring the sauce to the boil stirring continuously and boil for 3 minutes. Pour the sauce over the fish to serve.

	Chicken Stock	Wine Stock	Cider Stock
CALORIES PER PORTION:	150	200	180
CH UNITS PER PORTION:	$1\frac{1}{2}$	4	$2\frac{3}{4}$

Poached Fish au Gratin (for 2)

Prepare poached fish in a thick sauce as above. Just before serving, sprinkle 1 oz. grated cheese over the top of it. Put under a hot grill to melt and brown the cheese.

	Chicken Stock	Wine Stock	Cider Stock
CALORIES PER PORTION:	210	260	240
CH UNITS PER PORTION:	$1\frac{1}{2}$	4	$2\frac{3}{4}$

Above: poached fish au gratin. Below: salmon mousse

Salmon Mousse (for 2)

		Calories	CH units
1	Egg	90	0
1 teaspoon	Lemon juice	0	0
	Seasoning	0	0
¼ pint	Hot water	0	0
1 level teaspoon	Powdered gelatine	15	0
4 oz.	Fresh cooked or canned salmon, flaked	220	0
	Cucumber	0	0
		325	0

1. Separate the egg yolk from the egg white.
2. Beat the egg yolk with lemon juice and seasoning over hot water until it thickens.
3. Allow to cool, still beating. Add the gelatine dissolved in hot water and the flaked salmon.
4. Allow mixture to cool and thicken slightly. Whisk the egg white till stiff and fold into the mixture.
5. Pour mixture into individual moulds and allow to set for a couple of hours.
6. Remove mousse from moulds and garnish with cucumber.

CALORIES PER PORTION: 160
CH UNITS PER PORTION: 0

● *See illustration on previous page.*

Variations
Several other flaked fish can be used to make a mousse:

		Calories	CH units
Smoked haddock mousse	*4 oz. flaked smoked haddock*	90	0
White haddock mousse	*4 oz. flaked haddock*	90	0

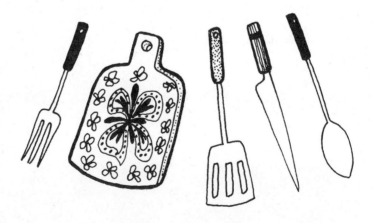

84

Spicy Mackerel (for 2)—Method 1

		Calories	CH units
2 (4 oz.)	Mackerel	240	0
1	Onion	15	$\frac{3}{4}$
2–3	Cloves	0	0
1	Bay leaf	0	0
12	White peppercorns	0	0
	Parsley	0	0
	Pinch thyme and mace	0	0
	Pinch salt	0	0
$\frac{1}{2}$ pint	Vinegar	10	0
		265	$\frac{3}{4}$

1. Clean and wash fish.
2. Cut off head and fins.
3. Lay in baking dish with finely sliced onion, spices, herbs and salt.
4. Cover with vinegar and bake in moderate oven (Gas Mark 3, 325°F., 163°C.) until thoroughly cooked (about 30–40 minutes).
5. Lift out fish into deep dish, strain the vinegar over them and serve when cold with salad.

CALORIES PER PORTION: 130
CH UNITS PER PORTION: $\frac{1}{2}$

● *See illustration overleaf.*

Spicy Mackerel (for 2)—Method 2

		Calories	CH units
2 (4 oz.)	Mackerel	240	0
2 oz.	Spring onions	10	$\frac{1}{2}$
	Pinch mixed herbs	0	0
	Seasoning	0	0
	Little milk	0	0
		250	$\frac{1}{2}$

1. Put a spring onion inside each mackerel. Add herbs and seasoning.
2. Roll and put in baking dish with a little milk. Cook in cool oven (Gas Mark 2, 300°F., 149°C.) until ready (about 40–50 minutes).

CALORIES PER PORTION: 125
CH UNITS PER PORTION: $\frac{1}{4}$

Spicy mackerel

Smoked Haddock in Savoury Sauce (for 2)

		Calories	CH units
8 oz.	*Smoked haddock*	160	0
½ pint	*Slimmers' savoury sauce*	40	1¾
	(see page 134)		
1	*Hardboiled egg*	90	0
	Worcester sauce	0	0
	Chopped parsley	0	0
		290	1¾

1. Trim the fish. Put into frying pan with water to cover and bring to boil. Simmer for 10–12 minutes, according to thickness of fish.
2. Lift out. Reserve stock to make sauce. Remove bones and place fish flakes into ovenproof dish.
3. Prepare Slimmers' savoury sauce and add finely chopped hardboiled egg and a few drops of Worcester sauce.
4. Pour sauce over fish and top with chopped parsley.

CALORIES PER PORTION: 145
CH UNITS PER PORTION: 1

Smoked Haddock Omelette (for 2)

		Calories	CH units
8 oz.	Smoked haddock	160	0
	Little milk	0	0
4	Eggs	360	0
2 oz.	Grated cheese	240	0
		760	0

1. Cook smoked haddock in little milk. Remove from milk and flake fish.
2. Make a plain omelette (see page 93) with the eggs and before quite ready spread over with the fish. Roll up quickly.
3. Sprinkle generously with grated cheese and brown under the grill. (Be sure not to overcook the omelette before adding the fish or it will be overdone with the extra grilling.)

CALORIES PER PORTION: 380
CH UNITS PER PORTION: 0

Baked Cod Fillet (for 2)

		Calories	CH units
2 (about 8 oz.)	Cod fillets	160	0
1	Onion	15	$\frac{3}{4}$
	Salt	0	0
Sauce			
Tin (about 8 oz.)	Tomatoes	40	2
$\frac{1}{2}$ teaspoon	Mustard	0	0
	Seasoning	0	0
		215	$2\frac{3}{4}$

1. Put cod in lightly greased pie dish or non-stick dish.
2. Cover with thinly sliced onion and sprinkle in seasoning.
3. Make mustard paste with the tomato juice and pour over fish together with the tomatoes.
4. Bake in moderate oven (Gas Mark 4, 350°F., 177°C.) for $\frac{3}{4}$ hour depending on thickness of fish.

CALORIES PER PORTION: 105
CH UNITS PER PORTION: $1\frac{1}{2}$

Shellfish Dishes

Because of the limited season in which shellfish are available and their comparative high cost, although many of them would make excellent low calorie meals they are not readily available to slimmers. Unless you are lucky enough to live near the coast, you will probably only be able to buy shellfish in quantities too small for a complete meal. However, they can certainly be used as the basis of many starters and also make tasty extras in sauces and stuffings (e.g. Prawn Stuffing, page 116, and Shrimp Sauce, page 136) or as garnishes. Here are some ideas for using shellfish in less fattening starters:

Shrimp Stuffed Tomatoes (for 2)

		Calories	CH units
4	*Large tomatoes*	60	3
About 3 oz.	*Shrimps, either fresh or canned*	90	0
	Lemon juice	0	0
	Black pepper	0	0
		150	3

1. Cut off the top of the tomatoes, scoop out the flesh and seeds and put in bowl.
2. Add shrimps, lemon juice and pepper to the bowl and chop coarsely while mixing with the tomatoes.
3. Pile mixture back into tomato cases and decorate each with a whole shrimp.

CALORIES PER PORTION: 75
CH UNITS PER PORTION: 1½

Variations
Prawns and scampi can be used in all these recipes instead of shrimps.

Shrimp Stuffed Courgettes (for 2)

Cook 2 medium sized courgettes (4 oz. each) in boiling water for 10 minutes. Cut out a wedge and fill with shrimp and lemon juice mixture. Garnish with slices of lemon.

CALORIES PER PORTION: 55
CH UNITS PER PORTION: 0

Shrimp Stuffed Peppers (for 2)

Blanch 2 green peppers in boiling water for 3 minutes. Cut in half, scoop out seeds and discard. Fill with shrimp and lemon juice mixture as before. Garnish.

CALORIES PER PORTION: 85
CH UNITS PER PORTION: 0

● *See illustration overleaf.*

Crabmeat Stuffed Tomatoes (for 2)

		Calories	CH units
4	Large tomatoes	60	3
2 oz.	Tinned crabmeat	70	0
	Lemon juice	0	0
	Black pepper	0	0
	Lettuce	0	0
		130	3

1. Prepare tomatoes and stuffing using crabmeat as in recipe on page 88.
2. Stuff tomatoes and serve on a bed of lettuce.

CALORIES PER PORTION: 65
CH UNITS PER PORTION: 1½

Variation
Lobster meat can be used instead of crabmeat.

● *See illustration overleaf.*

Shellfish Cocktails

A good prawn cocktail with a sauce which is reasonably low in calories and CH Units can be prepared (for 2) using the following ingredients:

		Calories	CH units
2 oz.	Cooked prawns	60	0
	Lettuce	0	0
Sauce			
¼ pint	Tomato juice	25	1
1 tablespoon	Lemon juice	0	0
1 teaspoon	Worcester sauce	5	0
2 tablespoons	Plain yoghurt	30	½
	Seasoning	0	0
		120	1½

1. Mix all the sauce ingredients until smooth.
2. Put prawns in individual dishes on a bed of lettuce leaves.
3. Cover prawns with sauce and chill until ready.

CALORIES PER PORTION: 60
CH UNITS PER PORTION: ¾

● *See illustration overleaf.*

Above: shrimp stuffed peppers. Below: crabmeat stuffed tomatoes

Prawn cocktail

Variations
More cocktails can be made by replacing the prawns with other seafoods as
follows:

		Calories	CH units
		per portion	
Shrimp cocktail	*2 oz. Cooked shrimps*	60	$\frac{3}{4}$
Crab cocktail	*2 oz. Flaked crabmeat*	65	$\frac{3}{4}$
Lobster cocktail	*2 oz. Flaked lobster meat*	65	$\frac{3}{4}$

Egg Dishes

Egg Naturelle

As has already been mentioned, eggs are one of the most useful foods for slimmers. If you like plain eggs for breakfast, here are some tips about cooking them in a low calorie way. The recipes that follow show you how you can use eggs in a variety of snack or supper dishes.

Boiled Egg

You cannot vary this recipe very much. Simply boiling an egg in water will not alter its calorie value (about 90 Calories for a large egg, 70 for a small one) and it contains no carbohydrate whatsoever.

Fried Egg

The egg does not need to swim in fat to produce a good fried egg. If you are using a non-stick pan, a knob of fat about the size of a walnut (about $\frac{1}{4}$ oz.) should be enough if you are careful not to let it burn. If you have a griddle, brush it over with a little oil, let the oil get hot and then break the egg on to it. When frying bacon at the same time, let some of the fat come out of the bacon into the pan. Pour away the excess fat carefully and then break the egg into the pan which should now be well covered in fat.

> 1 fried large egg (by any of above methods)=145 Calories (approx.)
> 0 CH Units

Poached Egg

If you have an aluminium poacher all you need to do is to melt a little fat (a small piece on the tip of a knife will do) so that the poaching cup is evenly coated and then pour away any excess. If you have a non-stick poacher, you probably will not even need this amount of fat, and with one that has plastic cups you can cook a perfect poached egg without any fat at all.

If you do not have an egg poacher, you might poach your eggs in boiling salted water with a few drops of vinegar. This is also a 'fatless' method of poaching. Stir the boiling water vigorously so that you make a 'well' and drop the egg into this.

Scrambled Egg (for 2)

The standard recipe for scrambled eggs suggests you use $\frac{1}{2}$ oz. margarine and 2 tablespoons (1 fl. oz.) milk to every two eggs – adding about 135 more Calories. You can cut down the fat to about $\frac{1}{4}$ oz., use low calorie milk, and still get good scrambled eggs. So if you are cooking scrambled eggs for two, do it this way:

		Calories	CH units
2	*Large eggs*	180	0
2 tablespoons (1 fl. oz.)	*Low calorie milk*	10	$\frac{1}{4}$
$\frac{1}{4}$ *oz.*	*Margarine*	55	0
		245	$\frac{1}{4}$

1. Break the eggs into a bowl and add milk. Beat together.
2. Melt fat in saucepan.
3. Add egg mixture and stir thoroughly until the eggs are completely 'scrambled'. Season to taste.

CALORIES PER PORTION: 120
CH UNITS PER PORTION: 0

Omelettes
Basic Recipe (for 2)

		Calories	CH units
4	*Eggs*	360	0
	Seasoning	0	0
$\frac{1}{4}$ *oz.*	*Margarine or 1 tablespoon oil*	55	0
		415	0

1. Break the eggs into a bowl and gently mix the yolks and whites using a fork. Add seasoning.
2. Melt the fat in a shallow pan and make certain that the bottom of the pan is well greased with hot fat.
3. Pour the egg mixture into the pan. The edges will immediately set because of the heat in the pan. Pull the set edges into the middle so that the raw mixture runs to the edges.
4. When most of the omelette is set, fold the mixture double and cook for another minute or so.
5. Serve and eat immediately.

CALORIES PER PORTION: 210
CH UNITS PER PORTION: 0

Variations on plain omelette

The following table gives some idea of the different flavours and stuffings you can add to a savoury omelette and tells you at what stage in the cooking they should be added. It also shows the increase in calories and CH Units per portion that must be allowed. You can of course use a couple of fillings together – cheese and tomato for example – and you are bound to discover your own variations. Incidentally, omelettes are a marvellous way of using up leftovers – cooked vegetables for instance.

You will find some ideas for making omelettes which are suitable as desserts on page 154.

Addition (per portion)	When to add	Increase in Calories per portion	Increase in CH Units per portion
1 oz. grated cheese	Before folding omelette	Approx. 100	0
1 tomato finely sliced	Before folding omelette	10	$\frac{1}{2}$
1 oz. prawns or shrimps	Before folding omelette	30	0
1 oz. cooked and flaked smoked haddock	Before folding omelette	20	0
1 oz. flaked tuna fish	Before folding omelette	75	0
1 oz. finely chopped onions and 1 crushed clove garlic	Before folding omelette	5	0
1 oz. streaky bacon (*gently fried in own fat*)	Before folding omelette	115	0
1 oz. finely chopped spinach	To egg mixture	5	0
½ small green or red pepper (*chopped*) *about 2 oz.*	To egg mixture	20	0
1 oz. chopped mushrooms (*gently poached in water, stock or lemon juice*)	To egg mixture	Negligible	0
1 tablespoon finely chopped fresh herbs (*parsley, chives, mint tarragon or chervil*)	To egg mixture	Negligible	0
1 oz. chopped lean ham	To egg mixture	60	0
1 oz. cooked chicken	To egg mixture	35	0

Above: soufflé. Below: eggs in a bed of spinach

Soufflé (Basic Mixture) (for 4)

		Calories	CH units
3	*Large eggs*	270	0
2 oz.	*Butter*	450	0
2 oz.	*Flour*	200	10
½ pint	*Milk made from dried, skimmed powder*	90	2¾
1 level teaspoon	*Made mustard*	3	0
	Seasoning	0	0
		1,013	12¾

1. Separate egg yolks and whites. Beat egg yolks together and whisk egg whites until stiff.
2. Melt the butter over a gentle heat.
3. Gently stir in the flour. Cook roux for few minutes and then add the milk gradually to form a smooth white sauce. Add mustard and seasoning.
4. Bring to the boil and cook for 3 minutes, stirring all the time.
5. Add egg yolks to the mixture. Stir well.
6. Fold in whisked egg whites thoroughly.
7. Transfer soufflé mixture to well greased soufflé dish and bake (Gas Mark 5, 375°F., 190°C.) for about 45 minutes.

CALORIES PER PORTION: 255
CH UNITS PER PORTION: 3¼

● *See illustration on page 95.*

Variations on basic soufflé
As in the case of omelettes, recipes for sweet soufflés are given in the section on desserts, page 154. The following table shows the additions necessary for some savoury soufflés and the number of calories and CH Units you must add. All additions must be added to the white sauce before adding the eggs.

Addition (per portion)	Increase in Calories per portion	Increase in CH Units per portion
1 oz. cottage cheese	30	0
1 oz. grated cheddar cheese	120	0
1 oz. cooked chicken	35	0
1 oz. cooked lean ham	60	0
1 oz. cooked chopped kidney	30	0
1 oz. cooked chopped veal	35	0
1 oz. cooked, flaked smoked haddock	20	0
1 oz. fresh or frozen shrimps	30	0
1 oz. tinned, drained sweetcron	25	1
1½ oz. fresh cooked or tinned asparagus (chopped)	10	0
1½ oz. chopped, poached mushrooms	3	0
1 tablespoon tomato purée or ketchup	20	1

Baked Eggs

The simple way to bake an egg is to break the egg into a greased baking dish (small tinfoil dishes are useful here) and to cook slowly for 10 minutes or so (Gas Mark 4, 350°F., 177°C.) until the egg just sets.

CALORIES PER PORTION: approx. 90–100
CH UNITS PER PORTION: 0

Variations on baked eggs
Instead of breaking the eggs directly into the dish, you can break them into holes in a savoury bed of cooked vegetables:

Eggs in a Bed of Spinach (for 2)

		Calories	CH units
8 oz.	Tinned or frozen spinach	40	0
2	Large eggs	180	0
		220	0

1. Put the spinach in an ovenproof dish and cook as given in the directions.
2. When nearly cooked, make a couple of holes and break the eggs into these. Continue baking (Gas Mark 4, 350°F., 177°C.) until the eggs are set.

CALORIES PER PORTION: 110
CH UNITS PER PORTION: 0

● *See illustration on page 95.*

Eggs in a Bed of Mushrooms and Celery (for 2)

		Calories	CH units
4 oz.	Mushrooms, chopped	8	0
4 oz.	Celery, chopped	12	0
	Seasoning	0	0
	A little stock	0	0
2	Large eggs	180	0
		200	0

1. Poach the mushrooms and celery with the seasoning in the stock until vegetables are soft. Pour off any excess liquid.
2. Put the vegetable mixture into an oven dish. Make two holes in mixture and break the eggs into these.
3. Bake for a further 10 minutes (Gas Mark 4, 350°F., 177°C.) until eggs are set.

CALORIES PER PORTION: 100
CH UNITS PER PORTION: 0

Eggs in a Bed of Chicken Livers (for 2)

		Calories	CH units
4 oz.	Chicken livers	160	0
¼ oz.	Fat	55	0
2 tablespoons	Tomato juice	5	0
2	Large eggs	180	0
	Seasoning	0	0
		400	0

1. Chop the chicken livers into small pieces and partly fry in the fat (no longer than 5 minutes).
2. Transfer to an ovenproof dish. Make a well in the middle and add the tomato juice.
3. Break the eggs into the well and sprinkle with seasoning.
4. Bake until the eggs are set (Gas Mark 4, 350°F., 177°C.).

CALORIES PER PORTION: 200
CH UNITS PER PORTION: 0

Variations
Instead of chicken livers, you can use:

	Calories per portion	CH Units per portion
4 oz. partly fried kidneys	180	0
4 oz. liver sausage	300	2
4 oz. cooked lean ham	240	0

Eggs on a Bed of Seafood (for 2)

		Calories	CH units
4 oz.	Shelled shrimps or prawns	120	0
2 tablespoons	Anchovy essence	20	1
2	Large eggs	180	0
6 (1 oz.)	Anchovy fillets	40	0
		360	1

1. Put the shrimps or prawns at the bottom of an ovenproof dish.
2. Pour the anchovy essence on top.
3. Break the eggs on top and bake until set (Gas Mark 4, 350°F., 177°C.).
4. Put the drained anchovy fillets on top in a criss-cross pattern and cook under a medium hot grill for a further 3 minutes.

CALORIES PER PORTION: 180
CH UNITS PER PORTION: ½

Stuffed Eggs with Mushroom (for 2)

		Calories	CH units
4	*Large eggs*	360	0
2 oz.	*Chopped mushrooms*	4	0
2 tablespoons	*Milk*	20	$\frac{1}{4}$
		384	$\frac{1}{4}$

1. Boil the eggs in salted water for 10 minutes.
2. Place in cold water immediately and allow to cool.
3. Remove shell and cut eggs in two, lengthways.
4. Poach mushrooms gently in the milk.
5. Take out the yolks and put in a bowl with the mushrooms and milk.
6. Mash with a fork and pile the mixture back into the egg whites.

CALORIES PER PORTION: 190
CH UNITS PER PORTION: negligible

Variations
Instead of the cooked, chopped mushrooms, you can mash the egg yolks with:

	Total Calories	Total CH Units
2 skinned tomatoes, chopped	190	$\frac{1}{2}$
4 oz. celery, chopped	185	0
2 oz. grated cheese	300	0
2 oz. flaked tuna fish	255	0
2 oz. tinned salmon	235	0
6 anchovy fillets, finely chopped	210	0

Floating Islands (for 2)

		Calories	CH units
4	*Large eggs*	360	0
2 oz.	*Grated cheese*	240	0
		600	0

1. Separate the yolks and whites of the eggs.
2. Whisk the egg whites until stiff.
3. Place the whisked egg whites on a greased pie dish and make four holes.
4. Put the egg yolks in the holes. Cover with grated cheese.
5. Bake for 15–20 minutes (Gas Mark 4, 350°F., 177°C.).

CALORIES PER PORTION: 300
CH UNITS PER PORTION: 0

Tomato Scramble (for 2)

		Calories	CH units
4	*Skinned tomatoes*	40	2
$\frac{1}{4}$ oz.	*Margarine*	55	0
2	*Large eggs*	180	0
	Seasoning	0	0
		275	2

1. Cut the tomatoes into small pieces and cook for a few minutes in the fat.
2. Beat the eggs and add the mixture to the tomatoes. Stir till creamy. Add seasoning to taste.

CALORIES PER PORTION: 135
CH UNITS PER PORTION: 1

Cheese Dishes

You will find plenty of recipes which use cheese in other parts of this book (e.g. Vegetables au gratin, page 116). However, here are a few ideas for using cheese in savoury and snack dishes:

Slimmers' Macaroni Cheese (for 2)

		Calories	CH units
2 oz.	*Uncooked macaroni*	200	9
½ pint	*Slimmers' cheese sauce (pouring) (see page 136)*	240	4
1 teaspoon	*Powdered mace or cinnamon*	0	0
1 oz.	*Grated cheese*	120	0
		560	13

1. Cook the macaroni in boiling, salted water till soft.
2. Drain in colander and wash through with hot water. Put into warmed ovenproof dish.
3. Make sauce (see page 136) and pour over macaroni.
4. Sprinkle with mace or cinnamon and grated cheese. Brown under a hot grill for a few minutes.

CALORIES PER PORTION: 280
CH UNITS PER PORTION: 6½

Cauliflower Cheese (for 2)

		Calories	CH units
1 (about 12 oz.)	*Cauliflower*	60	3
½ pint	*Slimmers' cheese sauce (see page 136)*	240	4
1 oz.	*Extra grated cheddar cheese*	120	0
		420	7

1. Trim and soak cauliflower in cold water for 15 minutes.
2. Place in boiling, salted water and simmer for about 20 minutes until tender but not broken.
3. Meanwhile make the sauce (see page 136).
4. Drain cauliflower and place in ovenproof dish.
5. Coat with cheese sauce.
6. Sprinkle with remaining cheese and brown under hot grill.

CALORIES PER PORTION: 210
CH UNITS PER PORTION: 3½

Cheese and Chive Scramble (for 2)

		Calories	CH units
3	Eggs	270	0
2 oz.	Grated cheddar cheese	240	0
1 teaspoon	Salt	0	0
Pinch	Cayenne pepper	0	0
1 oz.	Butter	225	0
1 tablespoon	Chopped chives (or onions if chives not in season)	0	0
		735	0

1. Beat eggs and add the grated cheese and seasonings.
2. Melt butter in saucepan. Add the egg and cheese mixture and cook over a gentle heat until lightly scrambled.
3. Add chopped chives. Serve hot.
   If using onion, cook for a while in the butter until soft before adding the egg mixture.

CALORIES PER PORTION: 365
CH UNITS PER PORTION: 0

Cheese Stuffed Peppers (for 2)

		Calories	CH units
2 (about 4 oz. each)	Peppers suitable for stuffing	80	0
1 oz.	Streaky bacon cut into small pieces	115	0
1 medium	Onion	15	$\frac{3}{4}$
2 oz.	Mushrooms, chopped	4	0
2 oz.	Grated cheese	240	0
4 oz.	Curd cheese	120	0
1 teaspoon	Chopped parsley	0	0
1 teaspoon	Mustard	0	0
	Seasoning	0	0
		574	$\frac{3}{4}$

1. Cut the top off peppers and remove seeds. Shave a piece off bottom so that they will stand easily.
2. Fry the bacon in its own fat, then fry onion and mushrooms.
3. Mix these together with cheese, parsley, mustard and seasoning and pack into the peppers.
4. Replace the tops of the peppers and put in baking dish.
5. Cover with greaseproof paper and bake in moderate oven (Gas Mark 4, 350°F., 177°C.) for 30–40 minutes.

CALORIES PER PORTION: 285
CH UNITS PER PORTION: negligible

Left: cheese stuffed peppers

103

Eggs and Cheese en Cocotte (for 2)

		Calories	CH units
6 oz. packet	Frozen spinach	30	0
2	Eggs	180	0
2 tablespoons	Milk	20	$\frac{1}{4}$
2 oz.	Grated cheddar cheese	240	0
	Seasoning	0	0
		470	$\frac{1}{4}$

1. Cook spinach as directed on packet. Drain and cool.
2. Divide between two individual dishes.
3. Break eggs into each dish and put 1 tablespoon milk on top of each. Season and sprinkle on grated cheese.
4. Place in shallow tin of warm water and bake in moderate oven (Gas Mark 4, 350°F., 177°C.) for 25–30 minutes.

CALORIES PER PORTION: 235
CH UNITS PER PORTION: negligible

Slimmers' Cheese Pie (for 2)

		Calories	CH units
2 (about 1 oz.)	Rashers bacon cut into small strips	115	0
2 oz.	Mushrooms, sliced	4	0
1	Small onion, grated	10	$\frac{1}{2}$
2 oz.	Hard cheese, diced very small	240	0
Pinch	Nutmeg	0	0
	Seasoning	0	0
2 teaspoons	Chopped parsley	0	0
2	Eggs	180	0
$\frac{1}{2}$ pint	Low-fat milk	95	$2\frac{3}{4}$
		644	$3\frac{1}{4}$

1. Cook the bacon in its own fat and cook the mushrooms in same fat for 3 minutes.
2. Add the grated onion, cheese, nutmeg, seasoning and parsley and mix together thoroughly.
3. Sprinkle this mixture on bottom of a greased baking dish.
4. Beat the eggs and add milk.
5. Pour this mixture into the baking dish.
6. Place baking dish in a deep tin containing enough water to come nearly to top. Cook in a cool oven (Gas Mark 2, 300°F., 149°C.) until the custard is set. This will take around 35–40 minutes.

CALORIES PER PORTION: 320
CH UNITS PER PORTION: $1\frac{3}{4}$

Tasty Cheese Snack (for 2)

		Calories	CH units
8 oz.	Curd or cottage cheese	240	0
1 tablespoon	Made mustard	10	0
2 tablespoons	Vinegar	1	0
2 tablespoons	Low-fat milk	10	$\frac{1}{4}$
		261	$\frac{1}{4}$

Plus any of these:
Worcester sauce, tomato ketchup, Yorkshire relish, horseradish sauce, any pickle or chutney, garlic or onion juice.

1. Soften cheese and work in mustard, vinegar, milk, until you have a thick purée.
2. Then add what you like of the other ingredients. Serve on toast or crisp-breads.

CALORIES PER PORTION (basic recipe): 130
CH UNITS PER PORTION: negligible

Tomato and Cheese Casserole (for 2)

		Calories	CH units
8 oz. tin	Tomatoes	40	2
8 oz.	Curd cheese	240	0
1	Egg	90	0
	Seasoning	0	0
	Pinch mixed herbs	0	0
1 teaspoon	Made mustard	0	0
		370	2

1. Drain tomatoes and cut into pieces; keep juice. Put a layer of these on bottom of greased dish and season well.
2. Sprinkle with curd cheese.
3. Repeat until cheese and tomatoes are used up.
4. Beat egg, add seasoning, herbs and mustard, and stir in a little tomato juice.
5. Pour over the cheese mixture.
6. Bake in moderate oven (Gas Mark 4, 350°F., 177°C.) for about 30 minutes or until firm.

CALORIES PER PORTION: 185
CH UNITS PER PORTION: 1

Left: French bean and cheese salad. Above: cheese puff. Below: slimmers' cheese dip

Cheesey Roes (for 2)

		Calories	CH units
$\frac{1}{2}$ lb.	Soft cod or herring roes	280	0
$\frac{1}{2}$ oz.	Flour	50	$2\frac{1}{2}$
	Seasoning	0	0
	Little fat	30	0
$\frac{1}{2}$ pint	Slimmers' cheese sauce (pouring consistency)	240	4
1 oz.	Grated cheese	120	0
	Chopped parsley	0	0
		720	$6\frac{1}{2}$

1. Wash and dry the roes.
2. Add pepper and salt to some flour and dip roes in mixture. Shake off the surplus flour.
3. Cook roes very gently in fat.
4. Blot off excess fat using absorbent paper and transfer to ovenproof dish.
5. Make the sauce (see page 136).
6. Pour sauce over roes and sprinkle grated cheese on top.
7. Brown under hot grill for a few minutes.
8. Garnish with chopped parsley before serving.

CALORIES PER PORTION: 360
CH UNITS PER PORTION: $3\frac{1}{4}$

Spanish Cheese (for 2)

		Calories	CH units
$\frac{1}{2}$ oz.	Butter	115	0
1	Medium onion, sliced	15	$\frac{3}{4}$
4	Tomatoes, skinned and sliced	40	2
3	Eggs, separated	270	0
4 oz.	Grated cheddar cheese	480	0
1 dessertspoon	Milk	10	0
	Seasoning	0	0
		930	$2\frac{3}{4}$

1. Melt butter in frying pan and fry onion until tender but not brown.
2. When nearly done add tomatoes and lightly cook.
3. Remove from pan and keep warm.
4. Whisk egg whites until stiff.
5. Beat egg yolks with 2 oz. grated cheese, milk and seasoning.
6. Fold cheese mixture into egg whites and pour into pan. Cook until underside is set and golden brown.
7. Place onions and tomatoes over the top and sprinkle the remaining cheese on top.
8. Cook under hot grill for 5 minutes until golden brown and well risen.

CALORIES PER PORTION: 465
CH UNITS PER PORTION: $1\frac{1}{2}$

French Bean and Cheese Salad (for 2)

		Calories	CH units
½ lb.	French beans	40	0
1 (4 oz.)	Red pepper, chopped	40	0
8 oz.	Cottage cheese	240	0
3	Hardboiled eggs, quartered	270	0
		590	0

1. Cook beans in boiling salted water until tender.
2. Arrange on dish with pepper, cheese and eggs.

CALORIES PER PORTION: 295
CH UNITS PER PORTION: 0

● *See illustration on page 106.*

Cheese and Cabbage Casserole (for 2)

		Calories	CH units
½ lb.	Shredded white cabbage	40	2
	Pinch salt	0	0
½ pint	Slimmers' cheese sauce, pouring consistency (see page 136)	240	4
1 level teaspoon	Made mustard	0	0
2 oz.	Grated Cheddar cheese	240	0
		520	6

1. Cook shredded cabbage in lightly boiling salted water until just tender.
2. Drain (keeping a little of the water to use in sauce).
3. Make sauce (see page 136). Add mustard to sauce.
4. Mix in the cabbage and turn all into ovenproof dish.
5. Sprinkle remaining 2 oz. of cheese on top and brown under a hot grill.

CALORIES PER PORTION: 260
CH UNITS PER PORTION: 3

Slimmers' Cheese Spread

Make a very tasty low calorie spread to put on crispbreads, etc. by blending savoury flavourings with curd cheese. Try your own combinations of the following flavourings; the spread will contain about 40 Calories an ounce:

    Lemon juice
    Clove of garlic, crushed
    Mixed herbs, fresh if possible – parsley, chives
    Cayenne pepper

Cheese and Banana Salad (for 2)

		Calories	CH units
2	*Bananas*	120	4
	Lemon juice	0	0
8 oz.	*Cottage cheese*	240	0
1 (about 6 oz.)	*Lettuce*	18	0
4	*Medium tomatoes*	40	2
	Watercress	0	0
	Chopped parsley	0	0
		418	6

1. Slice bananas finely and sprinkle with lemon juice.
2. Mix bananas with cottage cheese.
3. Pile cheese and banana mixture on to a bed of lettuce.
4. Garnish with sliced tomatoes, watercress and chopped parsley.

CALORIES PER PORTION: 209
CH UNITS PER PORTION: 3

Slimmers' Cheese Dip

You can make the following dip for parties. Resist the temptation yourself to dunk crisps in the dip by using sticks of celery and carrot:

		Calories	CH units
$\frac{1}{2}$ lb.	*Cheese (Edam or Cheddar is good)*	960	0
1 carton	*Plain yoghurt*	75	$1\frac{1}{4}$
2 tablespoons	*Low calorie salad cream*	50	0
Small tin (3 oz.)	*Tuna fish or pink salmon*	225	0
	(drain off excess oil)		
	Salt and pepper	0	0
	Little low-fat milk	0	0
		1,310	$1\frac{1}{4}$

1. Place all ingredients except milk into liquidiser goblet and run machine until smooth mixture obtained.
2. Add milk to make dip a good consistency (i.e. not too thick or it will be impossible to sample and not too thin or it will drop all over the place).

APPROXIMATE CALORIES PER DUNK: 10
APPROXIMATE CH UNITS PER DUNK: negligible

● *See illustration on page 107.*

Slimmers' Quiche (for 2)

		Calories	CH units
½ pint	Low-fat milk	95	2¾
2	Eggs	180	0
1 oz.	Hard cheese, grated	120	0
1 oz.	Cooked lean bacon	115	0
	Seasoning	0	0
		510	2¾

1. Beat milk and eggs together.
2. Stir in cheese, bacon and seasoning.
3. Pour into lightly greased basin and stand basin in small pan of water.
4. Bake in moderate oven (Gas Mark 4, 350°F., 177°C.) for about 30 minutes or until a knife inserted in the centre comes out clean.

CALORIES PER PORTION: 255
CH UNITS PER PORTION: 1½

Cheese Puffs (for 2)

		Calories	CH units
2	Average slices of bread	140	6
2	Egg yolks	150	0
2 oz.	Grated hard cheese	240	0
	Pinch mixed herbs	0	0
2	Egg whites	30	0
		560	6

1. Toast bread on one side only.
2. Mix egg yolks with grated cheese and mixed herbs.
3. Beat egg whites until stiff and then fold in cheesey mixture.
4. Pile on top of untoasted side of bread and grill until golden brown.

CALORIES PER PORTION: 280
CH UNITS PER PORTION: 3

● See illustration on page 107.

Vegetable Dishes

Vegetables can play an important part in a slimming diet because they provide bulk as well as vitamins and minerals without contributing too many calories or carbohydrates. Exactly how fattening they are depends on the part of the plant that is usually eaten. Stem and leaf vegetables (e.g. celery, lettuce, cabbage) contain very little carbohydrate while root vegetables (potatoes, carrots, turnips, parsnips) do contain more starch. When you are choosing vegetables to accompany a main course, remember the following:

1. The fresher the vegetables the better they are, as far as flavour and texture are concerned. Choose vegetables with contrasting colours if possible, e.g. carrots and peas.
2. Use the smallest possible amount of boiling salted water to cook the vegetables in. Do not presoak the vegetables and do not overcook them. This destroys their vitamin and mineral content.
3. Add extra flavour to vegetables by cooking with fresh herbs (see chart on page 140).

However, do not run away with the idea that vegetables must always play second fiddle to meat and fish when you are planning your meals. Here are some ideas of how vegetables can be used to their full potential, and add variety to your slimming meals. You can either try them as main dishes, snacks or starters. Alter your quantities accordingly.

Stuffed Vegetables

An endless variety of dishes can be prepared by stuffing vegetables, not only because many kinds are suitable for stuffing but also because an infinite number of different stuffings can be made, using almost any ingredient that you like to name. It is because a stuffing only calls for comparatively small quantities and the vegetables themselves are not terribly fattening that stuffed vegetables are one of the most useful dishes a slimmer can learn to cook. A basic recipe and then two tables are given below. The first table gives some idea of those vegetables which are suitable for stuffing and tells you how to prepare and cook them. The second table gives some ingredients you can use in the stuffings and suggests which of them are suitable for stuffing particular vegetables. Since there are so many permutations for the proportions of ingredients in the stuffing and the amount of stuffing relative to the vegetable, only the calories and CH Units per ounce of ingredient are included so that you can work out for yourself the total calories and CH Units in the dish of your choice.

Basic Recipe for Stuffed Vegetables

1. Clean and prepare the chosen vegetable for stuffing (see table). In some cases reserve the centre part to use in the stuffing (e.g. cabbage, tomatoes) ; in other cases (e.g. marrow) discard it.
2. If necessary, parboil the vegetable in salted water or bake it partially in the oven.
3. Mix together all the ingredients for the stuffing, season well and add herbs if liked, and fill the vegetable with it.
4. Cook as directed.

Table : Suitable Vegetables for Stuffing

Vegetable	Calories per oz.	CH Units per oz.	Preparation	Cooking
Aubergines	5	0	Blanch the aubergines by placing in boiling water for a couple of minutes. Cut in half lengthwise and remove the pulp. Add this to the rest of the stuffing and refill the aubergine cases.	Bake in a greased oven-proof dish and cook in a cool oven for 1 hour (Gas Mark 2, 300°F., 149°C.).
Cabbage	5	$\frac{1}{4}$	Choose a firm, white cabbage. Parboil in salted water for 10 minutes and then scoop out centre leaves to form a cavity. Chop up these leaves and use in stuffing if desired. Fill cavity with stuffing.	Bake in a greased oven-proof dish for at least 40 minutes or until cabbage is tender (Gas Mark 6, 400°F., 204°C.).
Courgettes	2	0	Wash courgettes and slit down one side. Cut out a wedge so that each courgette is like a boat. Parboil in salted water for 15 minutes. Fill with stuffing.	Cover stuffed courgettes with tinfoil and bake in a greased dish in a fairly hot oven (Gas Mark 6, 400°F., 204°C.) for about 1 hour or till tender.

Vegetable	Calories per oz.	CH Units per oz.	Preparation	Cooking
Marrow	2	0	Wash marrow and cut in half lengthwise. Scoop out pith and seeds. Either boil in salted water for 15 minutes, steam for 20 minutes or bake in moderate oven (Gas Mark 4, 350°F., 177°C.) for 30 minutes. Stuff both halves.	Cover stuffed halves with tinfoil and bake in a fairly hot oven (Gas Mark 6, 400°F., 204°C.) for about 30 minutes.
Peppers, green or red	10	0	Blanch the peppers in boiling water for a couple of minutes (this preserves the colour and makes it easier to remove seeds). Cut off top and remove seeds from inside. Stuff peppers through the top. *OR* Cut peppers in half lengthwise and stuff halves.	Place in an ovenproof dish and bake in a fairly hot oven (Gas Mark 6, 400°F., 204°C.) for about 30 minutes.
Potatoes	25	1	Wash, scrub and dry potatoes. Rub salt over the skin. Make a slit to prevent bursting. Bake in fairly hot oven (Gas Mark 6, 400°F., 204°C.) until tender (about 45 minutes to 1 hour depending on size). Cut in half lengthwise and scoop out insides. Add to rest of stuffing and refill potato cases.	Reheat in hot oven (Gas Mark 6, 400°F., 204°C.) for about 15 minutes.
Tomatoes	5	$\frac{1}{4}$	Choose large, well formed tomatoes. Cut off top and scoop out pulp. Add this to rest of stuffing and pile back into tomato cases.	Bake for 10 minutes in a hot oven (Gas Mark 7, 425°F., 218°C.). (No cooking needed if stuffed with cheese, salmon, crabmeat, etc.)

Left, above: stuffed cabbage. Below: stuffed courgettes

Suitable Stuffings for Vegetables

You will probably devise your own stuffings depending on what you have in your larder or fridge at the time (making stuffings is the perfect way of using up leftovers). You can use either cooked rice (35 Calories, 1½ CH Units per ounce) or breadcrumbs (70 Calories, 3 CH Units per ounce) as your base and add any of the following for flavour:

Stuffing flavouring	Calories per oz.	CH Units per oz.
Chopped, cooked meats, e.g. beef, pork, lamb	35–75	0
Cooked minced beef	75	0
Chopped, cooked chicken	35	0
Chopped, cooked liver or kidney	40, 30	0
Chopped, cooked ham	60	0
Chopped, cooked bacon	115	0
Tinned sweetcorn	25	1
Chopped, raw mushrooms	2	0
Chopped, raw onions	5	¼
Chopped, raw celery	3	0
Curd or cottage cheese	40, 30	0
Grated, hard cheese	120	0
Flaked, tinned salmon	40	0
Flaked, tinned tuna fish	75	0
Flaked, tinned crabmeat	35	0
Shellfish, e.g. prawns, shrimps	30	0
Chopped nuts, e.g. almonds	170	0
Puréed nuts, e.g. chestnuts	50	2
Chopped olives	25	0
Chopped gherkins	15	½
Chopped, hardboiled eggs	45	0

Recommended Combinations

Stuffing	Vegetable
Cooked rice, cooked meat and onions	Peppers, marrow, cabbage
Cheese and cooked ham	Tomatoes, potatoes
Cooked rice, sweetcorn and shrimps	Peppers
Breadcrumbs, onion, bacon and mushroom	Aubergines, courgettes
Tuna fish, salmon or crabmeat and onion	Tomatoes
Hardboiled egg, cheese and mushrooms	Tomatoes, potatoes
Cooked rice, mushrooms, onion and hardboiled egg	Marrow, courgettes

Vegetables au Gratin (for 2)

The combination of vegetables and cheese is a very pleasant one. You can prepare a variety of different dishes from the one basic recipe since the method is simply one of covering the cooked vegetables with a cheese sauce and finishing them off under the grill.

Basic Recipes

About 4 oz. cooked vegetable per person (see below).
$\frac{1}{4}$ pint coating cheese sauce per person.

Sauce

		Calories	CH units
$\frac{1}{2}$ oz.	*Cornflour*	50	$2\frac{1}{2}$
$\frac{1}{2}$ pint	*Separated milk (or made from low fat powder)*	95	$2\frac{3}{4}$
1 oz.	*Grated, hard cheese*	120	0
		265	$5\frac{1}{4}$
Extra 2 oz. grated cheese		240	0
$\frac{1}{2}$ oz. breadcrumbs		70	3
		575	$8\frac{1}{4}$

1. Cook the vegetable as shown in the table below and place in ovenproof dish.
2. To make the sauce, mix the cornflour with a little milk to a smooth paste. Heat rest of milk to boiling point and then pour on top of paste, stirring all the time. Return sauce to pan, add cheese and continue stirring for 3 minutes.
3. Pour the sauce over the vegetables. Mix the remaining grated cheese and breadcrumbs and sprinkle on top.
4. Put under hot grill for few minutes to brown.

CALORIES PER PORTION: 285
CH UNITS PER PORTION: 4

Suitable vegetable	Calories per oz.	CH Units per oz.	Preparation and cooking
Cauliflower	5	$\frac{1}{4}$	Wash and separate florets. Boil in salted water until tender.
Celery	3	0	Wash celery and cut into pieces about 6 inches long. Boil in a little salted water until tender.
Leeks	10	$\frac{1}{4}$	Wash leeks, cut into pieces about 2 inches long and boil in salted water until tender.
Marrow	2	0	Peel marrow, cut into rings about $1\frac{1}{2}$ inches wide. Remove pith and seeds from centre. Boil in salted water until tender.

● *See illustration overleaf.*

Celery au gratin

● *Tip. A quicker method for Vegetables au Gratin is to use a tinned or packet soup for the sauce instead of making a cheese one. Suitable flavours would be mushroom, thick onion, asparagus, celery, etc. Calorie and CH values would depend, of course, on the thickness of the soup but would be roughly 400 Calories and 10 CH Units for a pint at the most. So the value for the whole dish would be about the same once you have added a cheese and breadcrumb topping.*

Veg'n Egg Recipes

You can add extra flavour to vegetable dishes by serving the cooked vegetable with some form of eggs, either hardboiled, poached, baked or scrambled. Some recipes for baked eggs and vegetables are given on page 97. Here are some other ideas:

Vegetables with Scrambled Egg (for 2)

		Calories	CH units
$\frac{1}{2}$ oz.	*Butter or margarine*	115	0
4	*Eggs*	360	0
4 oz.	*Cooked, mixed vegetables*	80	2
	Seasoning	0	0
		555	2

1. Melt the fat in a pan.
2. Beat up the eggs and add, with vegetables and seasoning, to the pan.
3. Continue cooking until eggs are cooked.

CALORIES PER PORTION: 275
CH UNITS PER PORTION: 1

Vegetables with Poached Egg (for 2)

		Calories	CH units
2	*Large tomatoes*	30	$1\frac{1}{2}$
4 oz.	*Mushrooms*	8	0
4 oz.	*Mixed vegetables*	80	2
2	*Eggs*	180	0
$\frac{1}{2}$ pint	*Tomato soup*	150	4
		448	$7\frac{1}{2}$

1. Slice and grill the tomatoes and mushrooms.
2. Cook the mixed vegetables.
3. Mix all vegetables together.
4. Poach the eggs.
5. Put poached eggs on top of vegetables and pour heated tomato soup over the dish.

CALORIES PER PORTION: 225
CH UNITS PER PORTION: $3\frac{3}{4}$

Vegetables with Hardboiled Egg (for 2)
e.g. Cauliflower with Egg

		Calories	CH units
1 (say 10 oz.)	Medium cauliflower	50	2½
½ oz.	Butter	115	0
1 tablespoon	Vinegar	0	0
1	Hardboiled egg	90	0
	Salt and pepper	0	0
		255	2½

1. Cook cauliflower in boiling, salted water until tender. Keep warm in serving dish.
2. Heat the butter in pan until just turning brown, add vinegar and seasoning and pour this sauce over cauliflower.
3. Chop the egg and sprinkle over cauliflower before serving.

CALORIES PER PORTION: 125
CH UNITS PER PORTION: 1¼

Vegetable Casseroles

If you find you have got small quantities of quite a few different root vegetables you can make very tasty vegetable casseroles which are quite filling without being too fattening. The basic recipe uses onions, potatoes, carrots, turnips and parsnips. Other suitable vegetables for casseroles are tomatoes, marrow, aubergines, peas, broad beans, celery, leeks and mushrooms. The addition of a small quantity of bacon or ham will add to the flavour.

Basic Vegetable Casserole (for 2)

		Calories	CH units
½ oz.	*Fat*	115	0
2 oz.	*Bacon, chopped*	230	0
1 (5 oz.)	*Large onion, finely chopped*	25	1¼
1 (4 oz.)	*Medium potato, peeled and chopped*	100	4
2 oz.	*Carrots, finely chopped*	10	½
2 oz.	*Turnips, finely chopped*	10	½
2 oz.	*Parsnips, finely chopped*	30	1
½ pint	*Stock made from stock cube*	15	½
		535	7¾

1. Melt the fat and brown the bacon and chopped onion.
2. Add the rest of the chopped vegetables to the pan and sauté for a few minutes.
3. Add the stock and bring to the boil. Turn down heat, cover with lid and simmer for 20 minutes. Or, turn into a casserole dish and bake in a fairly hot oven (Gas Mark 5, 375°F., 190°C.) for about 30 minutes or until the vegetables are tender.

CALORIES PER PORTION: 265
CH UNITS PER PORTION: 4

Variations
Tomato Casserole

Use 8 oz. canned tomatoes instead of potatoes and keep tomato juice for stock.

CALORIES PER PORTION: 235
CH UNITS PER PORTION: 3

● *See illustration on page 122.*

Vegetables in Wine

Use ½ pint dry white wine as stock, omit bacon.

CALORIES PER PORTION: 240
CH UNITS PER PORTION: 5

Left: tomato casserole. Above: salade niçoise. Below: hot pepper salad

Salads

It is not surprising that salads are usually associated with slimmers since most salad vegetables are exceedingly low in calories and carbohydrates. If you want to slim and like salads you are halfway there. Salads are also useful to the slimmer for the following reasons:

- *You can eat an awful lot of salad at one sitting without doing yourself any harm. In other words, you can pile your plate high, take a long time to eat it and thereby not feel that you are cutting down on the amount of food you are eating.*
- *You can have an infinite variety of different salads to break the monotony of having the same thing each day.*
- *You can always have a side salad with a hot meal as an additional vegetable. This is a particularly useful trick if you are the only slimmer in a family eating larger quantities of meat, say, than yourself. You can then avoid that horrible feeling of finishing your meal before the others.*

This section contains some recipes which will be particularly useful during the summer when most of the vegetables are plentiful and cheap. Other recipes use vegetables that are available all the year round. I have tried to give you some idea of the variety you can get with salads, and even the most determined lettuce leaf hater might take a fancy to these. Each recipe gives quantities for four helpings as it is much easier to make the salads in bulk, keep them in the fridge and eat a portion as you want it. At the end of the section there are some ideas for low calorie salad dressings.

Salade Niçoise (for 4)

		Calories	CH units
4	Tomatoes	40	2
2	Hardboiled eggs	180	0
8–10	Anchovy fillets	60	0
8–10	Black olives	25	0
8 oz.	Cooked green beans	40	0
4 tablespoons	Lemon juice or vinegar	4	0
		349	2

1. Skin the tomatoes (stand in hot water for a minute or two), cut into quarters.
2. Cut the egg into quarters.
3. Blot anchovies with absorbent paper to remove excess oil and chop into small pieces.
4. Mix these and all other ingredients together. Add lemon juice or vinegar or any of the dressings on page 130 and shake in a bowl with a lid.

CALORIES PER PORTION: 90
CH UNITS PER PORTION: $\frac{1}{2}$

● *See illustration on page 123.*

Coleslaw (for 4)

		Calories	CH units
Small carton (5 oz.)	Natural yoghurt	75	$1\frac{1}{4}$
1 teaspoon	Made mustard (French or German, preferably)	5	0
1 teaspoon	Horseradish sauce	4	0
4 oz.	White cabbage, finely shredded	20	1
2 (8 oz.)	Large carrots	40	2
4 (8 oz.)	Small onions. finely chopped	40	2
	Salt and pepper to taste	0	0
1 tablespoon	Any fresh chopped herbs	0	0
		184	$6\frac{1}{4}$

1. Mix the yoghurt, mustard and horseradish sauce in a bowl.
2. Add all the other ingredients and mix thoroughly.
3. Season to taste.

CALORIES PER PORTION: 45
CH UNITS PER PORTION: $1\frac{1}{2}$

Continental Cucumber (for 4)

		Calories	CH units
1 (approx. 1 lb.)	Cucumber	48	0
3 tablespoons	Salt	0	0
	Lemon juice	0	0
	Ground black pepper	0	0
	Paprika pepper	0	0
		48	0

1. Peel the skin from the cucumber and slice the flesh finely.
2. Put cucumber in shallow dish and sprinkle the salt over it. Leave for 20 minutes for the water to seep out.
3. Pour away the water and press the cucumber firmly to release more water.
4. Add a drop of lemon juice to the cucumber and then sprinkle with black pepper and paprika.

CALORIES PER PORTION: 10
CH UNITS PER PORTION: 0

Cucumber Misère (for 4)

		Calories	CH units
1 (approx. 1 lb.)	Cucumber	48	0
2 fl. oz.	White vinegar	4	0
	Liquid sweetener to taste	0	0
		52	0

1. Peel the cucumber and slice the flesh finely.
2. Arrange attractively in a dish.
3. Pour the sweetened vinegar over the cucumber and leave 1 hour.
4. Serve as a side salad with cold or hot meat.

CALORIES PER PORTION: 15
CH UNITS PER PORTION: 0

Oriental Orange Salad (for 4)

		Calories	CH units
4	Medium oranges	160	10
4 (8 oz.)	Small onions	40	2
8–10	Black olives, stoned	25	0
	Small pinch coriander seeds	0	0
	Small pinch paprika	0	0
6 tablespoons	Lemon juice	12	0
	Salt and pepper	0	0
		237	12

1. Peel the oranges and slice them very thinly into a bowl.
2. Peel and chop the onions into fine rings – add to oranges.
3. Add the olives, coriander, paprika and lemon juice. Mix well.
4. Season to taste. Leave in fridge for 1–2 hours before serving.

CALORIES PER PORTION: 60
CH UNITS PER PORTION: 3

● Tip. Try as a side salad with liver and lamb dishes.

Oriental orange salad

Hot Pepper Salad (for 4)

		Calories	CH units
8 oz.	Celery	24	0
4 (1 lb.)	Red and green peppers	160	0
4 (8 oz.)	Finely grated small onions	40	2
8 tablespoons	Vinegar	16	0
2 drops	Tabasco sauce	0	0
		240	2

1. Finely grate all the vegetables or chop finely.
2. Add vinegar and Tabasco. Mix well.

CALORIES PER PORTION: 60
CH UNITS PER PORTION: $\frac{1}{2}$

● See illustration on page 123.
● Tip. You can add about 4 drops of liquid sweetener to this salad if you like.

Orange and Cauliflower Salad (for 4)

		Calories	CH units
1 (12 oz.)	Small cauliflower	60	3
4	Medium oranges	160	10
1 oz.	Chopped celery	3	0
	Lemon juice	0	0
	Salt and pepper	0	0
		223	13

1. Divide raw cauliflower into tiny florets.
2. Peel and chop orange into small pieces. Add to cauliflower.
3. Add celery and lemon juice.
4. Season to taste.

CALORIES PER PORTION: 55
CH UNITS PER PORTION: $3\frac{1}{4}$

Egg and Potato Salad (for 4)

		Calories	CH units
4 (about 1 lb.)	Medium sized potatoes	400	16
4	Hardboiled eggs	360	0
1 small carton (5 oz.)	Natural yoghurt	75	$1\frac{1}{4}$
Small bunch (2 oz.)	Watercress	10	0
3 teaspoons	Made mustard (French or German, preferably)	15	0
	Salt and pepper	0	0
		860	$17\frac{1}{4}$

1. Peel or scrape potatoes depending on age. Boil in salted water until just cooked. Drain and cut into small dice.
2. Chop hard boiled eggs and mix with potato.
3. Add yoghurt, chopped watercress and mustard.
4. Season to taste and leave in fridge until ready to serve.

CALORIES PER PORTION: 215
CH UNITS PER PORTION: $4\frac{1}{4}$

Jamaican Savoury Salad (for 4)

		Calories	CH units
1 (6 oz.)	Lettuce	18	0
4	Bananas	240	8
	Juice of half lemon	0	0
4	Tomatoes	40	2
		298	10

1. Wash, dry and tear the lettuce into small pieces. Arrange in the base of a bowl.
2. Peel and slice the bananas and mix with the lemon juice immediately. Pile in the centre of lettuce.
3. Slice tomatoes and arrange around edge of dish.

CALORIES PER PORTION: 75
CH UNITS PER PORTION: $2\frac{1}{2}$

Salad Dressings

If you buy ordinary salad cream in a bottle and have a tendency to drown your salad in it, you are most probably dressing your salad with more calories than the salad itself contains. (A tablespoonful contains about 115 Calories and $\frac{1}{2}$ CH Unit.) There are, however, a couple of special salad creams sold especially for slimmers nowadays, and using these will just about halve the calories you add. You could reduce this still further by mixing the slimmer's salad cream with an equal amount of vinegar. For those of you who would like to make your own salad dressings, here are some ideas:

Slimmers' French Dressing (for 4)

		Calories	CH units
2 tablespoons	Vinegar	4	0
$\frac{1}{2}$ tablespoon	Olive oil	130	0
$\frac{1}{2}$ tablespoon	Salt	0	0
$\frac{1}{4}$ teaspoon	Ground black pepper	0	0
$\frac{3}{4}$ teaspoon	Dry mustard	40	$\frac{1}{4}$
	Drop of liquid sweetener to taste	0	0
		174	$\frac{1}{4}$

1. Put all ingredients into small screw top jar.
2. Shake vigorously for a couple of minutes.

CALORIES PER PORTION: 45
CH UNITS PER PORTION: negligible

Cottage Cheese Dressing (for 4)

		Calories	CH units
2 oz.	Cottage cheese	60	0
	Juice of half lemon	0	0
	Salt and pepper	0	0
	Artificial sweetener to taste	0	0
		60	0

1. Blend the cheese and lemon juice together until smooth – either by sieving or using a liquidiser.
2. Add the seasoning and sweetener to taste.

CALORIES PER PORTION: 15
CH UNITS PER PORTION: 0

Right: yoghurt salad dressing

Tomato Juice Dressing (for 4)

		Calories	CH units
½ pint	Tomato juice (from a can of tomatoes if you like)	50	0
	Pinch dried tarragon	0	0
	Squeeze lemon juice or vinegar	0	0
	Small crushed clove of garlic (optional)	2	0
	Salt and pepper	0	0
		52	0

1. Mix all ingredients together, except for salt and pepper.
2. Season to taste.

CALORIES PER PORTION: 15
CH UNITS PER PORTION: 0

Yoghurt Salad Dressing (for 4)

		Calories	CH units
1 small carton (about 2 oz.)	Natural yoghurt	75	1¼
1 drop	Artificial sweetener	0	0
1 teaspoon	Lemon juice	0	0
1 tablespoon	French or German mustard	10	0
1 tablespoon	Parsley or gherkins, finely chopped	0	0
		85	1¼

Mix all ingredients together.

CALORIES PER PORTION: 20
CH UNITS PER PORTION: ¼

● See illustration on previous page.

Dressing the Salad

You will probably discover lots more dressings for yourself – the basic idea is to replace the usual olive oil by something like yoghurt, tomato juice or vinegar. When you are ready to dress the salad (just before serving, if you are dressing lettuce) you can either put your dressing in a bottle or jar with a sprinkler top or you can put salad and dressing in a bowl with a lid and shake up the whole lot so that the whole salad is nicely coated.

Gravies and Sauces

Some people find food unappetising if it is too dry so I have included the following section on low calorie gravies and sauces. Sauces can also be used to eke out leftovers such as cooked meat, fish and vegetables. A good sauce, even a low calorie one, can raise the dullest of leftovers to Cordon Bleu standard.

Thin Gravies

The section about roasting (page 43) mentioned that when you roast meat in foil or in roasting bags, all the meat juices and fats collect together in the foil or bag. If you pour off the liquid carefully and let it cool, the fat will float to the top. You can then remove it carefully from the meat juices, which you can reheat for your gravy, seasoning if necessary.

If you do not want to bother, or you want gravy for something other than a joint, you can make a quick thin gravy from a beef stock cube and water or from something like Bovril or Marmite and water. If you like a 'hot' gravy, try adding a couple of drops of Worcester sauce and/or a drop of Tabasco. Half a pint of gravy made in this way will not contain more than 10 Calories and will be free of carbohydrate.

If you like just a little more body in your gravy, you can always use the commercial gravy powders (e.g. Bisto). If you follow the directions on the packet you will make half a pint of gravy containing about 40 Calories and 1 CH Unit.

Sauces

The conventional method of making a pouring white sauce is to use 1 oz. fat, 1 oz. flour and 1 pint of milk (about 175 Calories or $1\frac{1}{4}$ CH Units per portion). If you like thick, coating sauces and use 2 oz. each of fat and flour to a pint of milk, a quarter pint 'dollop' will cost you about 255 Calories and $2\frac{1}{2}$ CH Units. So, whether you are cutting calories or carbohydrates it seems a good idea to think of some alternative ways of making sauces. The first few recipes here are all variations on the basic white sauce. These are followed by some recipes and ideas for other types of sauces.

Slimmers' White Sauce
Pouring Sauce (for 4)

		Calories	CH units
$\frac{1}{2}$ oz.	*Cornflour or arrowroot*	50	$2\frac{1}{2}$
1 pint	*Separated milk (or made from low-fat powder)*	190	$5\frac{1}{2}$
		240	8

Coating Sauce (for 4)

		Calories	CH units
1 oz.	*Cornflour or arrowroot*	100	5
1 pint	*Separated milk (or made from low-fat powder)*	190	$5\frac{1}{2}$
		290	$10\frac{1}{2}$

1. Mix the cornflour or arrowroot with about 1 tablespoon milk to a smooth paste.
2. Heat the rest of the milk to just below boiling point.
3. Add the milk to the paste, stirring all the time.
4. Return to the pan and stir until it has thickened to correct consistency.

N.B. If you do not have separated milk or low-fat milk powder, use $\frac{1}{2}$ pint milk plus $\frac{1}{2}$ pint water.

Pouring Sauce
CALORIES PER PORTION: 60
CH UNITS PER PORTION: 2

Coating Sauce
CALORIES PER PORTION: 70
CH UNITS PER PORTION: $2\frac{1}{2}$

Slimmers' Savoury Sauce (for 4)

		Calories	CH units
1 oz.	*Cornflour or arrowroot*	100	5
$\frac{1}{4}$ pint	*Separated or low-fat milk*	45	$1\frac{1}{4}$
$\frac{3}{4}$ pint	*Savoury stock (can use stock cube, fat free meat stock or vegetable stock)*	15	$\frac{1}{2}$
		160	$6\frac{3}{4}$

1. Mix a little cornflour or arrowroot with 1 tablespoon milk to a smooth paste.
2. Heat rest of milk plus stock to boiling point. Pour on to paste.
3. Return to pan. Stir until it thickens.

CALORIES PER PORTION: 40
CH UNITS PER PORTION: $1\frac{3}{4}$

Right: trout with pepper and tomato sauce

Slimmers' Egg Sauce (for 4)

			Calories	CH units
1		*Egg*	90	0
½ pint		*Separated or low-fat milk*	95	2¾
½ oz.		*Butter*	115	0
		Seasoning	0	0
			300	2¾

1. Put all the ingredients into a bowl above a saucepan of hot water.
2. Whisk or stir vigorously until you have a smooth sauce.

N.B. Do not let the water boil too vigorously or the sauce will curdle.

CALORIES PER PORTION: 75
CH UNITS PER PORTION: ¾

Variations on white, savoury and egg sauces
Once you have made a basic sauce, you can ring the changes by adding one or other of the following:

Sauce	Addition to one pint of sauce	Extra Calories per portion	Extra CH Units per portion
Anchovy sauce	1 tablespoon anchovy essence	2	0
Cheese sauce	2 oz. hard cheese, crumbled or grated	60	0
Cucumber sauce	4 oz. diced cucumber plus pinch of nutmeg	3	0
Egg sauce	1 hardboiled egg, chopped	20	0
Gherkin sauce	2 medium gherkins, finely chopped	4	0
Mustard sauce	1 tablespoon French or German mustard	2	0
Onion sauce	1 tablespoon dried onion flakes (pre-soaked in water)	2	0
Parsley sauce	1 tablespoon parsley, coarsely chopped	0	0
Seafood sauce	2 oz. cooked prawns or shrimps, chopped	15	0
Tomato sauce	2 tablespoons tomato purée	5	¼

Pepper and Tomato Sauce (for 4)

		Calories	CH units
2 (8 oz.)	Sweet peppers, green or red	80	0
8 oz.	Canned tomatoes, or 4 fresh tomatoes	40	2
2 tablespoons	Water, if using fresh tomatoes	0	0
1 tablespoon	Vinegar, wine if possible	2	0
2	Small gherkins, optional	0	0
	Salt and pepper	0	0
		122	2

1. Dip the peppers briefly in boiling water. Then remove seeds and stalks and cut them up into small pieces.
2. Skin and chop fresh tomatoes, if used.
3. Put tomatoes, peppers and water, if necessary, into pan and simmer for about 30 minutes or until pulpy.
4. Add the vinegar and sliced gherkins. Season to taste.

You can either serve the sauce like this or, if you like a more even texture, you can sieve the pulp or give it a few minutes in a liquidiser.

CALORIES PER PORTION: 30
CH UNITS PER PORTION: ½

● *See illustration on page 135.*

Yoghurt and Mint Sauce (for 4)

		Calories	CH units
	Few sprigs of fresh mint (or 1 teaspoon made up mint sauce)	0	0
1 carton (5 oz.)	Natural yoghurt	75	1¼
		75	1¼

1. If using fresh mint, chop it finely with a sharp knife.
2. Stir mint into the yoghurt.

This sauce is a particularly good one to serve with 'hot' dishes like curries.

CALORIES PER PORTION: 20
CH UNITS PER PORTION: ¼

Using Herbs, Spices and Seeds

When you are slimming you will almost certainly find that you are eating less food in bulk than you were before. So, what you must aim to do is to make the food that you do have as satisfying and tasty as possible. By including a good proportion of high protein foods such as meat, fish, eggs, cheese and milk in your diet, which you do automatically if you are carbohydrate cutting and which you are advised to do if you are calorie cutting, you should achieve *satisfying* meals since proteins keep you feeling satisfied longer than carbohydrates. As far as *taste* is concerned, you will find that the careful addition of herbs, spices and seeds can, on the one hand, completely transform a rather tasteless dish and, on the other hand, can help to bring out the natural flavour of the other ingredients.

There is no really clear distinction between herbs and spices. Roughly speaking however, most herbs are derived from the leaves of plants grown in a temperate climate while spices are derived from specific parts (e.g. stamens, bark, shells, etc.) of plants grown in tropical countries.

The chart that follows gives a very comprehensive list of herbs, spices and seeds and indicates in what sort of dishes they can be used.

A ●●● rating means that the herbs, spice or seed can definitely be used in that dish and the taste should be universally liked.

A ●● rating means that the combination of the herbs and dish will probably be a good one.

A ● rating means that the combination is one with which it is worth experimenting.

Where possible, it is always best to use fresh herbs which you can chop up just before adding to the pan and whole spices and seeds should also be crushed just before use. If you are starting your herbs and spice collection from scratch, you will probably do best to get the two standard mixtures, i.e. mixed herbs and curry powder, as your first buys. Mixed herbs are usually a mixture of parsley, sage, mint and thyme. The constituents of curry powder vary according to the maker but the spices most often used are coriander, turmeric, cumin, ginger, pepper, chillies and cardamon seed. Since dried herbs and spices lose their flavour after a while, it is advisable to keep them in airtight containers in a cool dark place and to buy in small quantities.

Left: herbs and spices

		Meat	Poultry	Game	Fish	Offal	Eggs
Allspice	S	●●●		●●●			
Anise seed		●●			●●		
Basil	H	●●					●●
Bay leaves	H	●●●	●●●				
Capers	H	●●	●●				
Caraway roots and leaves	H	●					
Caraway seed		●					
Cardoman seed							
Celery salt and seed	H				●●●		●●●
Cayenne	S				●●		●●●
Chervil	H				●●●		●●●
Chilli powder	S	●●●					
Chives	H	●●	●●				●●●
Cinnamon	S	●●●					
Cloves	S	●●				●●	
Coriander seed		●●	●●	●●			
Cumin seed		●●	●●				
Dill	H		●●		●●●		
Fennel					●●●		●
Garlic		●●●	●●●	●●●			
Ginger	S	●	●				
Horseradish	H	●●●			●●●		
Juniper seed		●●	●●	●●●			
Mace	S	●●		●●●			●●

Cheese	Salads	Vegetables	Stuffings	Sauces and soups	Marinades	Fruits
				●		●●
						●●●
●●		●●●				
				●●●	●●●	
				●●●		
	●●	●●●				
		●		●●		●●●
			●			●
	●●●		●●●			
●●●						
		●●		●●		
●●●	●●●	●●●	●●			
●						●●●
		●●		●●		●●●
			●●●			●●
						●
	●●	●●	●●●			
		●		●		
	●●●			●●●	●●●	
				●	●	●●●
				●	●●●	
●●				●●		●●

		Meat	Poultry	Game	Fish	Offal	Eggs
Marjoram	H	●●●			●●		
Mint	H	●●●			●		
Mustard seed		●●●		●●●			
Nasturtium seed							
Nutmeg	S	●●		●●		●●	●●
Onion salt		●					
Oregano	H	●●●	●●●	●●●			
Paprika	S	●●●	●●●			●●●	●●
Parsley	H	●●●	●●●	●●●	●●●		●
Poppy seed							
Rosemary	H	●●●	●	●●●	●		
Saffron	S						
Sage	H	●●●			●		●
Savory	H						
Sesame seed					●●		
Sorrel	H						
Tarragon	H	●●		●●●	●●		●
Thyme	H	●●	●●	●●●	●●●	●●	
Turmeric	S						
Vanilla pod							
Watercress	H	●●●	●●				

Cheese	Salads	Vegetables	Stuffings	Sauces and soups	Marinades	Fruits
●●				●●●		
						●●●
	●	●				
	●●					
				●●	●	
					●●●	
		●●				
		●●				
●			●●●			
●●		●●				●
		●●●		●	●●	
				●●		
	●	●●		●●	●●	
	●	●	●●●			
●●		●●				
		●●●				
				●		
		●●	●	●	●●	
		●●				
				●●●		●
		●●●		●●		

Desserts

I have included some recipes for desserts in this book for two reasons:

1. Quite a number of you will probably admit that it was your love of sweet things which made you fat. But whereas some of you will be able to cut out sweet things altogether when you realise how many calories and carbohydrates they contain, there are others who will not be able to make such a drastic change in one go. So, for you here are some suggestions for sweets which are comparatively non-fattening and which you can fit into your own calorie cutting or carbohydrate cutting diet as you please.

2. The best way to ensure that your children do not get fat is to make certain that while giving them adequate nutrients you do not overfeed them when they are young. Since children tend to have sweeter teeth than adults, it is particularly important not to encourage this love of sweet things to an extent where the child will only be satisfied with something sweet. Getting your children used to some of the less sweet desserts should help to train their palate.

If you want to work out your own less fattening sweets, base them on three things which are calorie free and therefore non-fattening however much you like to use. These are:

- *water*
- *air*
- *artificial sweeteners.*

The following recipes use lots of fresh fruit because of its high water proportion, gelatine because it is so useful for setting water and fruit juices, and eggs because they can be whisked and beaten to get the air into the dishes and give them their bulky appearance yet light texture.

Recipes using Fresh Fruit

In Chapter 6, I pointed out how most fruits contain a lot of water and that their calories arise mainly from their sugar content. They therefore make ideal foods for slimmers providing they are not sweetened by using lots of sugar.

Fresh Fruit Salad (for 4)

		Calories	CH units
2	Red eating apples	80	4
	Juice of one lemon	2	0
1	Orange	40	$2\frac{1}{2}$
1	Banana	60	2
1	Peach	40	2
2 oz.	Apricots	10	$\frac{1}{2}$
2 oz.	White or black grapes	30	2
$\frac{1}{4}$ pint	Water	0	0
	Liquid sweetener	0	0
		262	13

1. Core the apples and cut into segments leaving the peel on. Sprinkle with some of the lemon juice.
2. Peel the orange, banana, peach and apricots and cut into suitable sized pieces.
3. Halve grapes and remove pips.
4. Add rest of lemon juice to water and add liquid sweetener to taste.
5. Arrange fruit in bowl and pour liquid over it.

CALORIES PER PORTION: 65
CH UNITS PER PORTION: $3\frac{1}{4}$

● *See illustration overleaf.*

Variations
You can use more or less any fruit that you like depending on its availability. Try to aim, however, to get a good colour contrast between your fruits. You could use unsweetened fruit juices such as orange and grapefruit for your liquid and add artificial sweetener to this. The use of spices such as cinnamon, ginger and nutmeg and fresh herbs such as mint will greatly inprove the flavour of your fruit salad. You can make fruit salads look very impressive if you serve them in a scooped out melon (use the flesh of the melon in the salad).

Over page: fruit salads, fruit mousse

Stewed Fruits

When you stew fresh fruits remember that only a very small amount of water is needed in the pan because the fruit will make its own liquid. Always add artificial sweetener *after* cooking the fruit. If you are going to eat the stewed fruit by itself reserve most of the juice. If you are going to make a fruit fool, mousse or sorbet, form a fruit purée by getting rid of the excess water, using a sieve.

Fruit Fool (for 4)

Calories   CH units
see below

12 oz.	Soft fruit (e.g. plums, blackcurrants, blackberries, raspberries, strawberries, gooseberries, etc.)
	Little water
	Liquid sweetener
2 cartons (5 oz. each)	Natural yoghurt

1. Cook the fruit in the water to form a thick pulp.
2. Put fruit through a sieve or liquidise to form a purée.
3. Add liquid sweetener to taste. Cool.
4. Stir in the yoghurt and serve chilled.

Fruit	Calories per portion	CH Units per portion
Blackberries	65	$1\frac{1}{2}$
Blackcurrants	65	$1\frac{1}{2}$
Gooseberries	65	$2\frac{1}{4}$
Plums	65	$2\frac{1}{4}$
Raspberries	50	$1\frac{1}{2}$
Strawberries	50	$1\frac{1}{2}$

Fruit Mousse (for 4)

Calories   CH units
see opposite page

1 lb.	Soft fruit
	Liquid sweetener
	Little water
4	Egg whites

1. Make a fruit purée as for fruit fool.
2. Add liquid sweetener to taste.
3. Whisk egg whites until stiff.
4. Fold egg whites carefully into fruit purée.

● *See illustration on page 147.*

Fruit	Calories per portion	CH Units per portion
Blackberries	55	1
Blackcurrants	55	1
Gooseberries	55	2
Plums	55	2
Raspberries	35	1
Strawberries	35	1

Fruit Sorbet (for 4)

Use same quantities and fruits as for fruit mousse and, after folding in egg whites, put in shallow tray in ice compartment of refrigerator.

Fruit Cream (for 4)

		Calories CH units
1 lb.	*Soft fruit*	see below
	Little water	
4	*Egg yolks*	
	Liquid sweetener	
4	*Egg whites*	

1. Make a fruit purée as for fruit fool.
2. Beat the egg yolks and mix with the fruit purée.
3. Sweeten to taste, using liquid sweetener.
4. Whisk the egg whites until stiff.
5. Fold the egg whites carefully into the mixture.
6. Serve chilled.

Fruit	Calories per portion	CH Units per portion
Apples	130	2
Blackberries	130	1
Blackcurrants	130	1
Gooseberries	130	2
Plums	130	2
Raspberries	110	1
Strawberries	110	1

Baked Fruit (for 4)

The harder fruits such as apples, pears and bananas can be baked very success-fully without added fat using tin foil or roasting bags. Rather than use the rather fattening dried fruits as fillings, you can make tasty fillings with small quantities of fresh fruits.

		Calories	CH units
4	*Large apples or pears*	160	8
4 oz.	*Raspberries, blackcurrants or*	40	1
	blackberries (or mixture)		
	Liquid sweetener	0	0
		200	9

1. Wash, halve and core apples or pears.
2. Prepare soft fruit by washing and mixing if necessary. Pile into scooped out portions of apples or pears.
3. Place filled fruit in roasting bag or foil. Wrap and seal. Make a few slits in the roasting bag if used. Place bag or foil parcel in roasting tin.
4. Bake in fairly hot oven (Gas Mark 5, 375°F., 190°C.) for 30–40 minutes or until tender.
5. Reserve juices from bag or foil. Sweeten with liquid sweetener.

CALORIES PER PORTION: 50
CH UNITS PER PORTION: 2¼

Left: baked apples. Above: fruit jelly. Below: apricot fruit mould

Recipes involving Jelly or Gelatine

Fruit Jelly (for 2)—Method 1

		Calories	CH units
$\frac{1}{2}$ pint	Water	0	0
$\frac{1}{2}$ packet	Jelly cubes	210	$9\frac{3}{4}$
4 oz. Soft fruit (e.g. raspberries, blackberries)		40	1
		250	$10\frac{3}{4}$

1. Boil water and add to jelly cubes.
2. When dissolved add washed fruit.
3. Cool and put into refrigerator to set.

CALORIES PER PORTION: 125
CH UNITS PER PORTION: $5\frac{1}{2}$

Fruit Jelly (for 2)—Method 2

		Calories	CH units
1	Medium orange or grapefruit	40 or 30	$2\frac{1}{2}$ or $1\frac{1}{2}$
About $\frac{3}{4}$ pint	Water	0	0
$\frac{1}{2}$ in.	Cinnamon stick	0	0
2–3	Cloves	0	0
$1\frac{1}{2}$ level teaspoons	Gelatine	20	0
	Liquid sweetener	0	0
		60 or 50	$2\frac{1}{2}$ or $1\frac{1}{2}$

1. Grate the outside rind from the fruit, making certain not to grate the white pith. Squeeze the fruit to obtain juice. Make up to a pint with water.
2. Add grated rind, cinnamon stick and cloves to the liquid. Bring to boil and simmer for 5–10 minutes. Strain liquid through sieve.
3. Dissolve gelatine in a small amount of liquid (hold over boiling water) and then add rest of liquid.
4. Add liquid sweetener to taste, pour into mould or bowl and allow to set.

	Calories per portion	CH Units per portion
Grapefruit Jelly	25	$\frac{3}{4}$
Orange Jelly	30	$1\frac{1}{4}$

● See illustration on page 151.

Variations
You can make a milk jelly using either method. Use milk and water in the proportion 3 to 1. If you use some sort of low calorie milk (separated or made from skimmed low fat powder) you need to add an extra 45 Calories and $1\frac{1}{2}$ CH Units. If you use ordinary milk, add an extra 95 Calories and $1\frac{1}{2}$ CH Units.

Fruit Mould (for 4)

		Calories	CH units
1 lb.	*Soft fruit (e.g. gooseberries, raspberries, blackcurrants, redcurrants)*	see below	
	Liquid sweetener	0	0
½ oz.	*Gelatine powder*	50	0
2	*Egg yolks*	150	0
½ pint	*Milk, separated or skimmed low-fat*	90	2¾
2	*Egg whites*	30	0
	Colouring (optional)	0	0
		320+	2¾+

1. Purée fruit in a small amount of water.
2. Add liquid sweetener to taste and allow to cool.
3. Dissolve gelatine in a little hot water.
4. Heat milk and add the beaten egg yolks. Add dissolved gelatine and stir over low heat until mixture thickens. Cool.
5. Mix in the fruit purée and add colouring if used.
6. Whisk egg whites and fold into mixture.
7. Turn into mould and allow to set.

● *See illustration on page 151.*

	Calories per portion	CH Units per portion
Apricot mould	100	1¾
Blackberry mould	120	1¾
Blackcurrant mould	120	1¾
Gooseberry mould	120	2¾
Peach mould	120	2¾
Raspberry mould	100	1¾
Redcurrant mould	100	1¾

Recipes using Eggs

Sweet Omelettes and Soufflés

Pages 94 and 96 contained plenty of ideas for savoury omelettes and soufflés. Here are the basic recipes for a sweet omelette and soufflé and some suggestions for sweet flavourings and fillings.

Basic Sweet Soufflé Omelette (for 4)

		Calories	CH units
8	*Eggs, separated*	720	0
	Few drops liquid sweetener	0	0
1 drop	*Vanilla essence*	0	0
¼ oz.	*Margarine or 1 tablespoon oil*	55	0
		775	0

1. Beat egg yolks with sweetener and essence.
2. Beat egg whites until stiff.
3. Fold egg whites into yolk mixture.
4. Melt fat in pan and let it get hot.
5. Pour in egg mixture and let it cook for a couple of minutes without stirring so that the base cooks.
6. Transfer to hot grill and leave below grill for 2–3 minutes or until top is golden brown.
7. Fold in half, add filling if desired and serve at once.

CALORIES PER PORTION: 195
CH UNITS PER PORTION: 0

Above: hot sweet soufflé. Below: egg custard

Basic Hot Sweet Soufflé (for 4)

		Calories	CH units
3	Large eggs	270	0
2 oz.	Butter	450	0
2 oz.	Flour	200	10
½ pint	Milk, separated or made from low-fat skimmed powder	95	2¾
2 drops	Vanilla essence	0	0
	Liquid sweetener	0	0
		1,015	12¾

1. Separate egg yolks and whites. Beat egg yolks together and whisk egg whites until stiff.
2. Melt butter and stir in flour. Allow to cook for about 2 minutes. Add milk and vanilla essence gradually, stirring all the time as it thickens. Allow to boil for 3 minutes. Add filling at this stage if used.
3. Remove from heat and beat in egg yolks and sweetener.
4. Fold in whisked egg whites using metal spoon.
5. Transfer soufflé mixture to a well greased soufflé dish. Bake (Gas Mark 5, 375°F., 190°C.) for about 45 minutes.
6. Serve and eat at once.

CALORIES PER PORTION: 255
CH UNITS PER PORTION: 3¼

Suitable Fillings for Sweet Omelettes and Soufflés

Filling (for 4)	Extra Calories per portion	Extra CH Units per portion
2 oz. plain chocolate, flaked	75	1½
4 oz. almonds, finely chopped	170	0
2 bananas, mashed	30	1
4 oz. raspberries, crushed	5	¼
4 oz. strawberries, crushed	5	¼
Flesh from 2 oranges, finely chopped	20	1¼
Purée made from ½ lb. apples	20	1
Purée made from ½ lb. gooseberries	20	1
Purée made from ½ lb. blackberries	20	½
Purée made from ½ lb. blackcurrants	20	½
Purée made from ½ lb. damsons	20	½
Purée made from ½ lb. plums	20	1
Purée made from ½ lb. peaches	20	1
Purée made from ½ lb. apricots	10	½

Basic Egg Custard (for 4)

		Calories	CH units
3	*Eggs*	270	0
1 pint	*Milk, separated or made from low-fat powder*	190	5½
2 drops	*Vanilla essence*	0	0
8 drops	*Liquid sweetener*	0	0
	Nutmeg	0	0
		460	5½

1. Beat the eggs and put in ovenproof dish.
2. Heat the milk and essence to just under boiling. Add sweetener.
3. Add milk to egg mixture stirring as you do so.
4. Place dish in a tray of cold water, sprinkle with nutmeg and cook in a cool oven (Gas Mark 2, 300°F., 149°C.) for 1½ hours or until a skewer comes out clean when inserted.

CALORIES PER PORTION: 115
CH UNITS PER PORTION: 1¼

● *See illustration on page 155.*

Variation
Add a tablespoonful of finely grated lemon or orange rind with the milk to give a strong lemon or orange flavour.

Slimmers' Custard

By using low-fat milk and artificial sweetener for custard making, you can cut calories and carbohydrates quite drastically. To make 1 pint of custard, use the following quantities:

		Calories	CH units
1 oz.	*Custard powder*	100	5
1 pint	*Low-fat milk*	190	5½
	Artificial sweetener	0	0
		290	10½

1. Mix the custard powder to a smooth paste with about three tablespoonfuls of the cold milk.
2. Heat rest of the milk to just under boiling point and then pour milk on to paste.
3. Return custard to saucepan to thicken. Add artificial sweetener to taste.

CALORIES PER PORTION (¼ pint): 70
CH UNITS PER PORTION (¼ pint): 2½

Packed Meals

If you are a slimmer who is not at home all day what can you eat when the pangs of hunger hit you at midday? Well, of course, if you are in the habit of eating a substantial lunch anyway, say in a restaurant or firm's canteen, you might find it easier to make this your main meal of the day and have something lighter in the evening. If, however, you do not have time for a proper meal and usually just manage to snatch a quick snack, you will have to think carefully about what you eat when you work out how you can cut calories or carbohydrates. Very often, this snack, because of its convenience aspect, will be bulging with both calories and carbohydrates. As an example, consider this typical lunchtime snack:

	Calories	CH Units
Round of ham sandwiches		
2 slices of bread	160	7
½ oz. butter	115	0
1 oz. ham, lean and fat	145	0
2 chocolate biscuits	160	4
Apple, medium sized	40	2
	620	13

It would not take you very long to eat, but look at the large chunk of your calorie allowance it would take up – and it would definitely be your total for the day as far as carbohydrate was concerned if you were cutting carbohydrates. So, let us see what other ideas there are for quick midday snacks suitable for calorie and carbohydrate cutters.

Ready-packed Snacks for Slimmers

If you are one of those people who hardly have enough time in the morning to brush your teeth, let alone prepare some sort of packed meal, the ready-packed snacks for slimmers can solve your problem. Boots sell a whole range of these products, sweet and savoury, so you have a wide choice. Each packet tells you how many biscuits constitute a meal of about 300 or 400 Calories (see table below). Remember not to have anything else with these biscuits and not to eat more than one meal at a time. Replacing the lunchtime meal with a known calorie snack is useful in that you can work out just how much of your allowance you have left to spend on the evening meal.

Right: bought snacks: check their comparative calorie and carbohydrate contents overleaf

Bought Snacks

Still thinking of the slimmer who finds it easier to buy snacks at lunchtime, here are the Calorie and CH Unit values of things you can buy in a shop and eat straight away. Don't forget to count this snack when you add up your daily allowance.

Snack	Calories (approx.)	CH Units (approx.)
Natural yoghurt	75	$1\frac{1}{4}$
Fruit flavoured yoghurt	125	5
Ice cream, plain block (2 oz.)	110	2
Mini sausage roll (about $1\frac{1}{2}$ oz.)	150	2
Mini pork pie (about 2 oz.)	250	$3\frac{1}{2}$
Biscuit, plain	65	2
Biscuit, sweet	80	2
Piece of cake, plain fruit (about 2 oz.)	210	6
Piece of sponge cake (about 2 oz.)	170	6
Individual fruit pie	360	10
Apple, medium sized	40	2
Banana, medium sized	60	2
Orange, medium sized	40	$2\frac{1}{2}$
Peach, medium sized	40	2
Pear, medium sized	40	2
Cheese, cottage, 4 oz.	120	0
Cheese, curd, 4 oz.	160	0
Cheese, Cheddar, 2 oz.	240	0
Sweets, 1 oz.	95	5

Carbohydrate cutters who have a lunchtime snack problem will probably find that they take most of their 10 CH Units daily allowance at this time. An apple, orange and natural yoghurt add up to $5\frac{3}{4}$ Units. Cheese, of course, is a convenient food to have in a packed lunch but be careful that you have small quantities even though it is carbohydrate free. Because there are so many carbohydrate free dishes that you can make in the evening, it is not too disastrous if you do have some carbohydrate in your packed lunch as long as your total for the day is no more than 10 Units.

Do It Yourself Snacks

If you *do* have a little time to prepare something in the morning, there is much greater scope for your midday meal. Here are some ideas:

1. Hot soups make excellent fillers, particularly in the winter. Make half a pint of soup, put it in a vacuum flask and you will have a good hot start to your meal. A thin soup (e.g. chicken, noodle) will contain about 100 Calories (1–2 CH Units) and a very thick one (e.g. thick onion) about 200 Calories (4–6 CH Units).

2. Salads are easy to prepare and keep fresh in these days of polythene bags and airtight plastic containers. Use the ideas on pages 124 to 129 to add variety to the more conventional lettuce, tomato and cucumber salads. Most of the salad recipes given work out at less than 100 Calories a portion, e.g. hot pepper salad, oriental orange salad, orange and cauliflower salad. You can prepare reasonably large quantities of these salads, keep them in the fridge and take a portion every day. Your meal can be completed with about 200 Calories worth of a high protein food such as cold meat or cheese (2 oz. of each), a couple of hardboiled eggs or canned salmon or tuna fish (4 oz. of each).

3. If you want to make sandwiches, you can cut down the Calories and CH Units in them in the following ways:

a. Using special slimmers' bread instead of ordinary bread.
b. Using special slimmers' spreads such as Outline instead of butter or margarine.
c. Using low calorie crispbreads instead of bread.
    (One word of warning here – it is best not to make your crispbread sandwiches too long before you intend eating them because most fillings make the crispbreads anything but crisp if they are left in contact for too long.)
d. Using low calorie fillings which spread straight on to the bread or crispbread and therefore do not require butter or margarine, e.g. cottage or curd cheese, fish or meat paste, savoury spreads.
e. Making open sandwiches – using one slice of bread, toast or crispbread per sandwich instead of two. Suitable toppings for open sandwiches are:

> Cold meats
> Sardines and pilchards
> Salmon and tuna fish
> Hardboiled egg, chopped up with a few anchovies
> Shrimps and prawns on curd or cottage cheese.

Sliced or shredded vegetables – e.g. carrot, celery, radish, onion, tomato, cucumber – can all be added to give more flavour and colour contrast. Fresh herbs, too, have this effect. In fact, making open sandwiches is another ideal way of finishing up leftovers. If you have to make them in advance, pack the sandwiches with a layer of tinfoil or greaseproof between each, and wrap them all in tinfoil or put them in an airtight container.

4. If you have some limited form of cooking facility available at lunchtime, such as a single gas ring or electric plate, you can either heat up portions of meals that you have prepared yourself such as stews or casseroles (see pages 48 to 51) or you can buy some of the convenience tinned, frozen or dehydrated meals. On the next page are some examples:

Meal		Calories (approx.)	CH Units (approx.)
Smoked haddock (*boil in bag*)	8 oz. pack	215	0
Fish fingers	each	50	1
Frozen beefburgers	each	160	1
Frozen chicken rissoles	each	140	$2\frac{1}{2}$
Frozen sliced beef in gravy	5 oz. pack	155	$\frac{1}{2}$
Frozen steaklets	each	270	1
Tinned spaghetti bolognese	$7\frac{1}{2}$ oz. tin	150	$5\frac{1}{2}$
Tinned beef ravioli with tomato and cheese sauce	$7\frac{1}{2}$ oz. tin	215	7

If calorie cutters steer clear of meals which involve batter, breadcrumbs, thick sauces, etc., they should be able to find several hot 200-Calorie meals which they can cook in one saucepan. Carbohydrate cutters should stick to the meals which consist of meat or fish only, e.g. smoked haddock.

CHAPTER NINE

Day Plans

THIS CHAPTER consists of suggested plans for typical 1,000 Calorie and 10 CH Unit days for those of you who want some guidance about planning meals when you are slimming.

There are 10 complete days of meals of approximately 1,000 Calories. Then, there are 10 days of meals containing less than 10 CH Units for carbohydrate cutters. You can, of course, stick rigidly to these meals and go back to Day 1 after Day 10 so that you have a 10 day rota. You may prefer to follow the plans for 10 days only to get used to your diet and from then on make up your own menus. The Day Plans can also be used to simply provide you with ideas for breakfasts or for snack meals which can then be fitted into the days as you fancy them. There is no reason at all why you should ever eat anything you do not like when you are slimming — if you do not want smoked haddock for breakfast, have something else instead.

Although most fruits and vegetables can be bought in frozen form these days it is ridiculous not to buy them fresh when they are in season. In the plans fruits and vegetables have been put into three groups depending on their calorie content to enable you to make a sensible choice:

Group A (about 5 Calories an ounce)

Apricots	Artichokes	Chicory	Spinach
Grapefruit	Asparagus	Courgettes	Spring greens
Lemon	Aubergine	Cucumber	Swedes
Loganberries	Beans, runner	Lettuce	Tomatoes
Melon	Broccoli	Marrow	Turnips
Raspberries	Brussels sprouts	Mushrooms	Watercress
Redcurrants	Cabbage	Mustard and cress	
Rhubarb	Carrots	Onions	
Strawberries	Cauliflower	Parsley	
Tangerines	Celery	Radishes	

Group B (about 10 Calories an ounce)

Apples	Oranges	Bean sprouts
Blackberries	Peaches	Beans, broad
Blackcurrants	Pears	Beetroot
Cherries	Pineapple	Leeks
Damsons	Plums	Parsnips
Gooseberries		Peppers
Grapes		
Greengages		

Group C (more than 20 Calories an ounce)

Bananas	Beans, baked
Prunes	Beans, butter
	Peas
	Potatoes
	Sweetcorn

Some vegetables, like potatoes and onions, are included in the meals because it is assumed that they are available most of the year.

The Day Plans are arranged in such a way that recipes are given for using up leftover meat from a roast joint or poultry which you have on Days 1 and 8 on the carbohydrate-counted plans and Day 7 on the calorie-counted plans. So if you like your Sunday roast, start the calorie-counted plans on a Monday and the carbohydrate-counted plans on a Sunday.

No drinks have been included in these plans. Remember that water, black coffee, black tea and low calorie drinks are virtually calorie free but that you must allow accordingly for milk and sugar (if taken) in drinks. If you use low-fat milk and artificial sweetener, then you do not have to worry too much about limiting your fluid intake.

Calorie Counted Day Plans

Day 1

Breakfast	Calories
1 small glass unsweetened orange juice	60
Boiled egg	90
1 piece of toast, lightly buttered	100
	250

Snack meal	
3 fish fingers, grilled	150
3 oz. Group C vegetable (e.g. peas)	60
$\frac{1}{2}$ tin tomatoes	20
1 apple	40
	270

Main meal	
4 oz. chicken piece, grilled	140
3 oz. cooked rice	105
2 oz. Group C vegetable (e.g. sweetcorn)	40
4 oz. Group A vegetable (e.g. green pepper)	20
$\frac{1}{4}$ pint mushroom soup for sauce	100
1 portion fruit mousse (see page 148)	55
	460
TOTAL:	980

Day 2

Breakfast	Calories
1 grapefruit (unsweetened or using artificial sweetener)	30
1 portion scrambled egg	120
1 grilled tomato	10
1 piece of toast, lightly buttered	100
	———
	260

Snack meal	
1 mini pork pie	250
2 oz. Group A vegetable (e.g. celery)	10
4 oz. Group B or C fruit (e.g. banana)	80
	———
	340

Main meal	
1 portion kidneys in oxtail sauce (see page 64)	250
4 oz. boiled or mashed potatoes	100
4 oz. Group A vegetable (e.g. runner beans)	20
	———
	370
	———
TOTAL:	970
	———

Day 3

Breakfast	Calories
1 piece (4 oz.) smoked haddock	80
1 poached egg	90
	———
	170

Snack meal	
1 portion omelette with fresh herbs (see page 94)	210
4 oz. Group A vegetable (e.g. cucumber and watercress)	20
1 crispbread, lightly buttered	40
2 oz. curd cheese	80
	———
	350

Main meal	
1 portion basic meat casserole (see page 48)	400
2 oz. Group A vegetable (e.g. brussels sprouts)	10
2 oz. Group B vegetable (e.g. broad beans)	20
4 oz. boiled potatoes	100
	———
	530
	———
TOTAL:	1,050
	———

Day 4

Breakfast   **Calories**
1 oz. cornflakes or other cereal   100
¼ pint milk   95
Artificial sweetener   0
                                                        ───
                                                        195

Snack meal
Grilled gammon rasher (3 oz.)   270
4 oz. Group A vegetable (e.g. mushrooms)   20
4 oz. fresh fruit, Group A or B (e.g. peach)   40
                                                        ───
                                                        330

Main meal
1 portion fish cutlets in foil parcel (see page 77)   160
4 oz. Group C vegetable (e.g. baked beans, sweetcorn)   80
4 oz. potatoes   100
1 fruit flavoured yoghurt (5 oz.)   125
                                                        ───
                                                        465
                                                        ───
                               TOTAL: 990
                                                        ───

Day 5

Breakfast   **Calories**
2 oz. grilled lean bacon   230
2 oz. grilled tomatoes   10
                                                        ───
                                                        240

Snack meal
Grated cheese (2 oz.) on lightly buttered toast   340
4 oz. Group A fruit (e.g. rhubarb)   20
                                                        ───
                                                        360

Main meal
1 portion liver casserole (see page 63)   215
4 oz. Group A or B vegetable (e.g. carrots)   40
4 oz. cooked pasta (e.g. noodles)   120
2 oz. ice cream   110
                                                        ───
                                                        485
                                                        ───
                               TOTAL: 1,085
                                                        ───

Day 6

Breakfast	Calories
1 small glass tomato juice	25
1 poached egg	90
1 piece toast, lightly buttered	100
	215

Snack meal	
4 oz. cottage cheese or 1 oz. Cheddar cheese	120
4 oz. Group A vegetable (e.g. tomato, cucumber)	40
1 piece crispbread, lightly buttered	40
1 portion fruit jelly (see page 152)	125
	325

Main meal	
5 oz. grilled rump steak	375
4 oz. Group A vegetable (e.g. broccoli)	20
3 oz. potatoes	75
4 oz. Group A or B fruit, stewed	40
	510
TOTAL:	1,050

Day 7

Breakfast	Calories
1 kipper (about 4 oz.)	120
1 piece bread, lightly buttered	100
	220

Snack meal	
1 portion vegetables au gratin (see page 116)	285
4 oz. Group A vegetable (e.g. runner beans)	20
	305

Main meal	
½ pint thin soup (e.g. chicken noodle)	75
4 oz. roast beef	300
2 oz. boiled potatoes	50
4 oz. Group A or B vegetable (e.g. carrots, peas)	40
	465
TOTAL:	990

Day 8

Breakfast	Calories
2 pieces lightly buttered toast	200
½ oz. marmalade	40
	240

Snack meal	
3 oz. cold lean meat	225
2 oz. boiled potatoes	50
4 oz. Group A or B vegetables (e.g. brussels sprouts, swedes)	40
4 oz. Group B fresh fruit (e.g. apple)	40
	355

Main meal	
1 portion chicken casserole (see page 60)	345
2 oz. Group A vegetable (e.g. runner beans)	20
1 crispbread, lightly buttered	40
2 oz. curd cheese	80
	485
TOTAL:	1,080

Day 9

Breakfast	Calories
Slice cold lean ham (2 oz.)	120
2 tomatoes	20
	140

Snack meal	
2 oz. grilled cod roe	70
Piece lightly buttered toast	100
	170

Main meal	
½ avocado pear with one portion Slimmers' French dressing (see page 130)	170
1 portion Slimmers' cottage pie, using beef (see page 69)	405
4 oz. Group A or B vegetable (e.g. cabbage, spring greens)	40
1 portion fresh fruit salad (see page 145)	65
	680
TOTAL:	990

Day 10

	Calories
Breakfast	
½ grapefruit	15
1 portion plain omelette (see page 93)	210
	–––
	225
Snack meal	
½ pint clear soup	50
1 piece crispbread	30
3 oz. crabmeat	105
4 oz. mixed salad vegetables (Group A)	20
1 fl. oz. low calorie salad cream	50
4 oz. fresh fruit (Group B) (e.g. pineapple)	40
	–––
	295
Main meal	
1 portion beef risotto (see page 68)	265
4 oz. Group A vegetable (e.g. carrots, tomatoes)	20
4 oz. baked fruit (Group B) (e.g. apple)	40
1 portion Slimmers' custard (see page 157)	70
	–––
	395
	–––
TOTAL:	915
	–––

Carbohydrate Counted Day Plans

Day 1

Breakfast	CH Units
1 (5 oz.) carton natural yoghurt with	$1\frac{1}{4}$
4 oz. fresh fruit (Group A)	1
	$2\frac{1}{4}$

Snack meal	
1 portion stuffed eggs with mushrooms (see page 99)	0
4 oz. Group A or B vegetable	1
2 oz. cheese	0
2 crispbreads, lightly buttered	2
	3

Main meal	
6 oz. roast meat	0
4 oz. Group A vegetable	1
$\frac{1}{4}$ pint gravy	$\frac{1}{4}$
1 portion basic hot sweet soufflé (see page 154)	$3\frac{1}{4}$
	$4\frac{1}{2}$
TOTAL:	$9\frac{3}{4}$

Day 2

Breakfast   CH Units
  1 grilled pork sausage $1\frac{1}{2}$
  2 oz. grilled mushrooms   0
                                                                           $1\frac{1}{2}$

Snack meal
  4 oz. cold meat   0
  4 oz. Group A vegetable   1
  1 portion fruit mould (see page 153) $1\frac{3}{4}$
                                                                           $2\frac{3}{4}$

Main meal
  1 portion baked herrings with vinegar sauce (see page 76) $\frac{3}{4}$
  4 oz. Group A vegetable   1
  1 fruit flavoured yoghurt   5
                                                                           $6\frac{3}{4}$

TOTAL: 11

Day 3

Breakfast   CH Units
  1 boiled egg   0
  2 crispbreads, lightly buttered   2
                                                                           2

Snack meal
  Lean pork chop (4 oz.)   0
  4 oz. Group A vegetable (e.g. tomatoes)   1
  2 oz. potatoes   2
  4 oz. Group A fruit (e.g. slice of melon)   0
                                                                           3

Main meal
  $\frac{1}{2}$ pint thin soup   2
  1 portion cheese soufflé (see page 96) $3\frac{1}{4}$
  4 oz. Group A vegetable (e.g. tomatoes, mushrooms) 1
                                                                           $6\frac{1}{4}$

TOTAL: $11\frac{1}{4}$

Day 4

	CH Units
Breakfast	
½ grapefruit (using artificial sweetener)	¾
	¾

Snack meal	
3 fish fingers, grilled (3 oz.)	3
4 oz. Group A vegetable (e.g. lettuce, tomatoes, watercress)	1
2 oz. potatoes	2
	6

Main meal	
1 portion Slimmers' kebabs, maximum 6 oz. (using meat and vegetables)	0
4 oz. Group B vegetable (e.g. peppers)	2
2 crispbreads, lightly buttered	2
2 oz. cheddar cheese (or any cheese)	0
	4
TOTAL:	10¾

Day 5

	CH Units
Breakfast	
Piece smoked haddock (4 oz.)	0
	0

Snack meal	
1 portion ham omelette (see page 94)	0
4 oz. Group A or B vegetable	1
4 oz. Group B fruit (e.g. apple, orange, banana)	2
	3

Main meal	
1 portion liver casserole (see page 63)	2¼
2 oz. cooked rice	3
2 oz. Group A or B vegetable	½
1 natural yoghurt (5 oz.)	1¼
	7
TOTAL:	10

Day 6

	CH Units
Breakfast	
1 portion scrambled egg (see page 93)	0
1 piece toast, lightly buttered	$3\frac{1}{2}$
	$3\frac{1}{2}$
Snack meal	
1 piece cod fillet (4 oz.) grilled	0
2 oz. potatoes	2
4 oz. Group A vegetable (e.g. spinach)	1
	3
Main meal	
1 piece (6 oz.) gammon steak with pineapple	0
4 oz. Group B vegetable	2
2 oz. ice cream	2
	4
TOTAL:	$10\frac{1}{2}$

Day 7

	CH Units
Breakfast	
2 oz. grilled lean bacon	0
1 poached egg	0
2 grilled tomatoes	1
	1
Snack meal	
$\frac{1}{2}$ pint clear soup	1
2 oz. cheese	0
1 medium sized apple	2
	3
Main meal	
1 portion veal fricassée (see page 51)	$4\frac{1}{2}$
4 oz. Group A vegetable	1
4 oz. fresh fruit (Group A) (e.g. strawberries)	1
	$6\frac{1}{2}$
TOTAL:	$10\frac{1}{2}$

Day 8

Breakfast   CH Units
  1 kipper (4 oz.)   0
                                                                 ___
                                                                   0

Snack meal
  ½ pint onion soup   2
  1 portion basic vegetable casserole (see page 121)   4
  4 oz. fresh fruit (Group B)   2
                                                                 ___
                                                                   8

Main meal
  4 oz. roast meat or poultry   0
  2 oz. roast potatoes   2
  4 oz. Group A vegetable   1
                                                                 ___
                                                                   3
                                                                 ___
                                                      TOTAL: 11
                                                                 ___

Day 9

Breakfast   CH Units
  4 oz. lean ham   0
  1 poached egg   0
                                                                 ___
                                                                   0

Snack meal
  Grilled cod roes (4 oz.)   0
  Piece of lightly buttered toast $3\frac{1}{2}$
                                                                 ___
                                                                   $3\frac{1}{2}$

Main meal
  1 portion basic meat loaf (see page 67) $\frac{1}{2}$
  2 oz. cooked pasta   3
  4 oz. Group A or B vegetable (e.g. broad beans, spring greens) 1
  ½ grapefruit, artificially sweetened $\frac{3}{4}$
                                                                 ___
                                                                   $5\frac{1}{4}$
                                                                 ___
                                                      TOTAL: $8\frac{3}{4}$
                                                                 ___

175

Day 10

Breakfast   CH Units
  1 poached egg   0
  2 rashers lean bacon   0
  Grilled tomato   ½
                                                             ½

Snack meal
  4 oz. grilled liver   0
  4 oz. Group A vegetable   1
  4 oz. stewed or baked fruit (Group A or B)   1
                                                             2

Main meal
  1 portion salmon mousse (see page 84)   0
  1 portion coq au vin (see page 61)   5½
  4 oz. Group A vegetable   1
                                                             6½

                                     TOTAL: 9

CHAPTER TEN

Slimming the Family

The Overweight Child

Two rather alarming facts have emerged in the last few years. First, recent research has shown that fat babies are likely to become fat children who are most likely to become fat adults. Secondly, recent surveys have shown that there are more fat children now than ever before. So unless steps are taken at this stage it looks as though there will be even more fat people in the next generation than there are today. This is why I want to cover two aspects of the problem in this chapter: prevention and cure.

Starting from Birth

Thank goodness the number of 'Bonny Baby Contests' at last is dying out. The last thing that a mother should be encouraged to do is to make her baby big and plump. A healthy baby is one that is firm, pink and active — not one that lies gurgling passively like an overgrown marrow in its pram. Here are some tips so that you can make sure that your baby is healthy:

- *Do not forget that the amount of weight a baby gains is much smaller after the first weeks or so. Do not force feed your baby just so that he gains a lot of weight each week.*
- *Always keep to the amount of food that your doctor has recommended. Do not add an extra spoonful of food or cup of milk just for luck.*
- *When you switch your baby from liquid to solid foods remember to reduce the amount of liquids as you increase the amount of solids.*
- *Do not add a lot of sugar to any bottle feed unless there is some medical reason for it.*

At School Age

A child who is old enough to go to school will be just at the age where he will start having more say in what he eats. Even if he still eats all his main meals at home, it is quite likely that he will be offered titbits at school and will have a chance to spend his pocket money at the sweet shop. This is the time, then, when you must watch closely for any danger signs and do your best to teach him good eating habits at home. If he does have a chance to eat away from home, either at school or with a friend or relative, he will have some idea of the foods he can eat freely and those he must eat with caution. The best thing that you can do to encourage these good habits is to make a low carbohydrate diet seem a natural way of life in your family. Here are some ideas:

- *Never resort to sweets and biscuits as a method of keeping a child quiet. Encouraging a sweet tooth at this age could not only ruin his figure later on, but also his teeth.*

- *If you notice friends and relatives (grandparents are often the worst offenders) giving your child lots of sweet things, have a quiet word in the appropriate ear and point out how they could undo all your good work.*

- *Always give your child a small helping of anything to start with. If he likes it and eats it up he can then ask for more and it is then up to you to decide whether he can have it. Never press him to have an extra helping just because you want to finish something up.*

- *Keep your child active and occupied. Not only will this ensure he uses up a good amount of energy, but he will be less likely to hanker after food if his mind is on something else.*

- *Do not feel mean if you deny your child something. We all know that when a child says, 'Everyone else has . . .' he is usually only talking about one or two at the most. If either you or your husband have a weight problem, there is a good chance that your child will have inherited the tendency to gain weight easily – so reassure yourself by thinking of the trouble you will save him later on. In fact, as soon as he is old enough, explain how too much of the wrong sorts of food can make you fat. If you have slimmed successfully yourself, show him some old photographs taken when you were fat and tell him how much better you have felt since you have been slim.*

And now a final word of warning to mothers of young children. Never be tempted to eat up any food left by the family. Many mothers find this a reason for weight gain especially when the children are small and are just trying new dishes. The food may be delicious and it may have taken a long time to prepare but it is still better to throw it away or give it to the cat.

Slimming children who are already too fat

If your child is already too fat, the first thing you should do is to find out why this is so – sometimes an unhappy child will eat more than usual – or a child who wants to become popular at school will buy sweets for his friends and himself.

If there is no specific problem and you know that your child is fat because he has eaten too much over quite a long period, now is the time for you to do something about it. If you do not, a vicious circle could set in: the child will get fatter so he will be more likely to move about less and then he will get even fatter. The fatter he gets, the more he will have to suffer the torments and leg pulling of his schoolmates – this could seriously affect his progress at school and his ability to get on with others.

178

What you must do is to gently coax him to eat less of the high carbohydrate foods like biscuits, sweets and ices, and to replace these with lots of good protein foods like meat, fish and eggs. At the same time, think of ways to encourage him to get more exercise. This does not have to be energetic games of football — something which gives him lots of walking is just as good. Encourage him to explore his own neighbourhood, whether in the town or country. In this way he could discover new interests to occupy him and take his mind off food. Here are some ways that might help you to keep your child on a carbohydrate cutting diet:

- *Find out which of the high protein foods he likes best. Then use your imagination to serve up meat, fish, eggs, cheese, etc. in lots of appetising ways. One of the things that give sweet foods 'kiddie appeal' is their mouth-watering properties. Try to make your child's meals as attractive as possible, even if it does take more time.*

- *Encourage him to watch his weight go down. If he is old enough to know how to draw graphs, suggest that he has a graph hanging in his bedroom and marks his weight on it each week at the same time.*

- *Give him lots of incentives to lose weight — extra pocket money, new clothes, special trips or even allowing him to stay up a little later in the evening.*

- *If you have got other children who are not fat at the moment, it will not do them any harm at all to eat the same type of low carbo-hydrate meals as the child who has to lose weight. After all, the low carbohydrate diet is one of the healthiest ways of eating. It will be much easier for the fat child to resist temptation if sweet biscuits and cakes are never even on the table. And, of course, this applies to both parents too. You cannot expect your child to stick to his diet if both of you are tucking into jam doughnuts in front of him.*

The Overweight Husband

A recent survey of slimmers has confirmed a couple of facts which many of you have probably already noticed about men slimmers: (a) they are more likely than women to become fat in later life (more women are fat right from child-hood) and (b) when they make up their minds to slim they are more successful than women. So, there is a good chance that if you can persuade your over-weight husband to slim, he will succeed.

There are probably two main reasons why men are successful: the first medical, the second social. Without going into too much detail, scientists who have looked at hundreds of overweight people have found that people who have been fat since childhood find it harder (but not impossible) to lose weight compared with people who have got fat in the years after adolescence. Since women are more likely to have got fat earlier than men, this could be one reason. The other reason is that men usually have different motives for slimming than women. Rather than for reasons of looks or fashion, they are much more likely to be frightened into slimming by the realisation that their fatness could endanger their health and shorten their life.

This chapter, then, is not written for those men who have already been motivated into slimming as they can use the information in the rest of the book to help them. It is written particularly for the wife who can see that spare tyre of fat gradually inflating around her husband's midriff. If you are lucky, a gentle request might be all that is needed to get him to look at this book. If your warnings fall on deaf ears, you will have to resort to slightly different tactics. Here are some words of advice:

- *From your own experience and from what has been said on pages 16–19, decide whether he should be cutting carbohydrates or calories. As a general rule, most men are probably better suited to carbohydrate cutting – so, if you cannot decide, I suggest you start with this method.*

- *In most cases, the two meals that you eat together will be breakfast and dinner. Even if you have no control over what he eats at lunch or in between meals, you can make a start by carefully planning breakfast and dinner. If you succeed in reducing the amount of carbohydrate and fat he eats then, you might be able to reduce his total for the whole day to a level where he begins to lose weight. If not, you will have to take an interest in what he eats and drinks when he is not at home.*

- *If you decide to make your husband a carbohydrate cutter, it might be a good idea to spoil him a bit by giving him his favourite high protein foods for the first few weeks. If he likes juicy steaks, make sure he has a good large one – then he might not notice that he has got an extra vegetable or a side salad but no chips. If he has been used to cereal and toast in the morning, tempt him with a delicious cooked breakfast of lean bacon, poached or scrambled eggs, grilled tomatoes, etc. (remembering to keep your food as free of fat as possible). The great asset of the carbohydrate cutting method is that you can always make the plate look full – an enormous psychological benefit.*

- *If you have decided to make your husband cut calories, you can still do this in a way that will not seem too painful to him. If you use some of the low calorie methods of cooking on page 42, you should make quite a saving on his day's total.*

- *If your husband has a very sweet tooth, see if you can get him to use sugar substitutes (or, better still, give up sugar in drinks completely). If he has always said he dislikes saccharin, put some sweetener in his tea or coffee one day without telling him. If he notices the difference then, it would be cruel to force it on him – but if he does not, then you have definitely scored a point. All the pellet sweeteners are now 100 per cent saccharin but the granular sweeteners are saccharin-coated sugar – you might find that these would be a good compromise.*

- *If your husband is used to having very big or very stodgy meals at lunchtime, you will have to deal with this problem. I suggest that you wait until you have been cutting his carbohydrates or calories at home for some time before you mention this subject. If you have managed to get him used to less sweet and starchy foods or smaller portions, you might find that he has already changed his lunchtime eating habits along the same lines.*

● *If it has not happened that way, you could use a form of bribery to persuade him to have less for lunch. Make the evening meal as large as possible in bulk (but not in calories and carbohydrates) and you can then truthfully persuade him to save himself for a special evening meal.*

● *Lunchtime or after-work drinking is another problem for men slimmers. A couple of pints of bitter at 360 Calories and 17 CH Units makes rather a big item in any diet. There are three easy ways in which he can cut down the fat he gets from alcohol. The first is to visit the pub less frequently, the second is to drink less calorific drinks (spirits and wine rather than beer) and the third is to stick to his usual drinks but to cut down the amount he drinks at one time.*

● *Another difference between men and women slimmers that was seen in the survey mentioned above was the fact that men are more likely to use some form of increased exercise when they want to slim. Although this is a very good principle, some men are deceiving themselves if they really think that half an hour's squash a week will undo the damage done by several years' overeating and over-drinking. The comparative merits of different forms of exercise are discussed in the following chapter (page 182) but at this point let me stress that regular mild exercise is much better than irregular and strenuous exercise. If your husband uses lifts all the time, persuade him to use the stairs; if he drives everywhere, persuade him to incorporate an hour's walk somehow everyday (not necessarily all at the same time — four fifteen-minute walks would be just as good). Medical experts agree that this form of exercise is far better for a man who is not used to strenuous activities — not only for burning up a few extra calories but also for improving his circulation and preventing any threat of heart trouble.*

CHAPTER ELEVEN

Exercise and Slimming

Can Exercise Help You Slim?

DIET AND EXERCISE go together as methods of losing weight, yet while the effectiveness of diet is generally recognised, that of exercise is often questioned. It is sometimes argued, for instance, that exercise uses up calories so slowly that to try to lose weight by it is impractical. Quoted as support for this argument is the fact that a person walking at three miles per hour must walk for 14 hours (i.e. for 42 miles) to lose just one pound in weight (3,500 Calories).

This kind of argument, however, fails to take account of two things. First, if someone wished to lose weight by exercise alone, he or she would be advised to do it by walking at a faster pace than 3 m.p.h. Second, as weight control is achieved only if food 'input' and work 'output' are balanced, then the best results cannot be obtained by attending merely to diet (input). Output must also be controlled and the only reasonable way to control this is through exercise.

Lack of exercise is an important factor contributing to excess weight. Regardless of weight most people take less and less exercise as they grow older. Fat people, however, seem to be appreciably less active than the average person. Studies have shown that very fat workers in industry on average walk each day barely half the distance covered by their thinner workmates. Very fat women are less active still, and cover little more than one-third of the daily distance covered by women in general. Even when playing games it has been found that fat people rest, on average, twice as long as other players.

This inherent idleness may be hard for some fat people to accept. They will be only too conscious of the efforts they already make in moving about and cannot take kindly to others telling them they are idle. They should not, however, dismiss the above findings too casually. They *may* not be underactive, but the probability is that they are. And changing their exercise habits could be an important step towards recovering their youthful shapes.

This chapter suggests four ways in which you might change your exercise habits and provides four schedules for you to follow:

- Walking schedule (see page 186),
- Running schedule (see page 188),
- Home and Office Exercises (see page 192),
- Sports schedule (see pages 225 and 226).

How Effective is Exercise?

Just how effective exercise really is in keeping down weight may be judged by looking at the tables of the daily energy requirements of adults, published by the Department of Health and Social Security, 1969. From these tables it can be seen that active adults need almost one and a half times as much food per day (3,600 Calories) as do sedentary adults (2,600 Calories). So 1,000 Calories a day are used up in exercise by active adults – the equivalent of 104 lb. of fat per year.

Moreover the manual worker, to whom the figures for active adults applies, does not normally work at anything like the intensity at which a person would expect to work while deliberately taking exercise. For example, the entire 1,000 Calorie daily difference between the intake requirement of the manual worker and that of his sedentary workmate can be used up in only two hours of running, or in five or six hours of determined walking.

Competitive athletes can certainly consume calories rapidly. For example, in the 1971 London to Brighton Walking Race, two international race walkers were found to have lost 15 lb. and 13 lb. respectively – and the race lasted less than 9 hours ! This works out at a weight loss of about $1\frac{1}{2}$ lb. per hour. Although water loss undoubtedly accounted for an important proportion of this weight reduction, water balance checks showed that it did not account for all of it and it is clear that in their case exercise was an effective method of reducing weight.

Of course the overweight housewife cannot be expected to exercise as severely as the competitive athlete. Quite modest daily exercise, taken regularly, can tax her energy resources enough to produce the slimming and fitness benefits she requires.

Hypokinetic diseases (those arising as a result of inactivity) have established a place for themselves in medical literature. The importance of exercise in helping to reduce the spread of cardiovascular disease, a disease to which fat people are particularly prone, is reflected in the increasing frequency with which exercise is now prescribed, even for quite severely affected cardiac patients.

What Are Good Slimming Exercises?

Good slimming exercises should meet four basic requirements : they must be vigorous, enjoyable, sensible and regular. Let us consider each one of these criteria in turn, for they reflect the principles that have been used to construct the exercise programmes that follow.

1. Vigour

If an exercise does not involve vigorous work, which at best should involve the whole body, then it cannot have a slimming effect. For instance, isometrics, which are static strengthening exercises, have negligible slimming effects. The more work that is done, obviously, the greater are the slimming effects. There are four ways of increasing the work output : ·

- lifting heavier loads (e.g. moving the whole body rather than just parts of it),

- moving greater distances (e.g. walking further, lifting or jumping higher),
- increasing speed,
- continuing for longer.

2. Enjoyment

If you pick exercises you enjoy then you will be more likely to keep exercising, and so reap the full benefits. You can enjoy the performance of a particular movement, or enjoy the satisfaction of completing a demanding task. You can enjoy the novelty of an activity you have not tried before, or at least recently, so it helps to introduce variety into an exercise programme – trying out new activities and returning regularly to old ones.

3. Sense

Your slimming programme should suit your fitness, abilities and age. You may still *feel* capable of youthful activity, but may no longer possess the necessary suppleness, so take care to avoid sudden movements requiring maximum effort. Calf and hamstring muscles, for instance, are particularly prone to injury. Even if still strong, they will be stiffer and less able to relax and absorb shocks, so a sudden effort can tear them.

A schedule must start gently and progress slowly. You then have a chance to keep a check on your ability to cope with each level of work output in turn. The simple rule is that if you have no difficulty with one level of exercise then, after training a little at that level, you should be quite capable of coping with the next.

4. Regularity

Slimming exercises should be carried out regularly. Just as it is necessary when dieting to follow a fairly strict daily regimen, so also is it important to adhere to a regular daily exercise routine. Merely dabbling in exercise will produce exactly the same results as a half-hearted approach to diet – a disappointing failure to reduce. It is nonetheless unrealistic to assume that you will never miss a session of exercise, so it is sensible to arrange a compromise schedule of three, or perhaps four, exercise sessions a week. Such an arrangement can be effective, fit in with your other commitments and avoid feelings of guilt at having missed a day's workout.

Walking and Running Schedules

The walking schedule is intended to appeal to those who prefer to take their exercise at a slow and gentle pace, the running schedule for those who prefer a quicker return on their exercise investment. Both can be modified to suit those who prefer activities such as swimming, cycling or rowing.

Three basic types of exercise sessions are used in both walking and running schedules – the Even Pace, the Varying Pace and the Stop-Go versions.

The Even Pace Session

The entire workout period is devoted to exercise at a constant speed. This type of session is used exclusively during the first two weeks of any schedule and thereafter regularly at least once or twice each fortnight.

For the first week the speed chosen should be only moderately faster than your habitual pace, and the distance covered not much more than about 50 per cent further than you might normally expect to walk at any one time. After this the exercise load may be made heavier by increasing:

- the speed
- the distance
- the duration

of the walking or running work. Keep a record of your speed and the distances you cover so that you may control your progress.

The Varying Pace Workout

In the varying pace workout the available time is divided into three phases:

i. *a warm-up phase* lasting about five minutes,
ii. *a high-intensity phase* during which the speed of walking and running is varied at pre-determined intervals between a high speed that you cannot maintain for long (Main Intensity Work), and a slower speed to give you time to recover (Secondary Intensity Work).
iii. *a tapering-off phase* of about five minutes of very light effort.

In the high-intensity phase of the workout, you may change speed gradually between the main and secondary levels over a period of a minute or more, or you may change suddenly over two or three paces. But once you have changed your pace, you must maintain your new speed for between twenty seconds and five minutes, depending upon the intended effort.

You can progress by increasing:

- the speed,
- the distance,
- the duration,
- the number of repetitions of each work unit.

The Stop-Go Workout

Often called 'Interval Training', this is an extension of the varying pace workout.

The session is divided into warm-up, main activity and taper-off phases as before. The main phase should consist of a succession of fast runs or walks over a fixed distance. These bursts of activity should be punctuated by short periods of rest. These should normally last from one to two minutes, but may be as short as five seconds or may even be extended to five minutes. The repeated phases may cover a constant distance – e.g. six 440-yard walks, making a total of 1½ miles. Alternatively, you could increase or decrease the distance pyramid-fashion – e.g. four 220-yard walks, plus two of 440 yards, plus one of 880 yards.

You can progress as before by increasing speed, the number of repetitions and the distance covered, or by decreasing the resting time between repetitions.

The Stop-Go workout is an effective element in slimming training, which should appeal to the well organised and energetic.

Walking

Walking is so familiar and gentle an exercise that you may never have regarded it as a method of losing weight. Certainly when compared with a vigorous activity like running it may appear to be of little importance, but its value should not be underrated. You can keep going over longer distances, with greater effect than you might imagine.

Walking is convenient. You need no special facilities and no special clothing; you may become hot but not excessively so, for there is time to dissipate your heat gradually.

It is unobtrusive — you can go for a daily walk without having to run the gauntlet of wisecracks or curious stares from neighbours.

In the schedule that follows, walking is not regarded as a single activity, but as a whole family of activities. This family is presented in Table 1 together with the calorie costs of each type of walk. These costs are calculated for a standard individual weighing eleven stone (154 lb./70 kg.) walking on a firm surface. Individuals differ, of course, and these standard values should be considered *only as a guide* to the energy costs of walking. There are many reasons why people differ in their calorie expenditure, even though engaged in identical activities. Skill and general efficiency are particularly important, but the most important factor is body weight. The heavier you are, the more calories you use for a given work task.

These energy expenditure figures apply to walking on a flat firm surface. If your walking is done on any other sort of surface, the calorie costs of your walk will rise and you should allow for this. For instance, walking in soft snow may increase your energy expenditure by as much as 40 per cent. Even walking on wet grass may raise it by 15 per cent.

Due allowance must also be made for the gradients up which you walk, for walking up or down hill is obviously more costly than walking on the level. At a walking speed of 3 m.p.h. a 10 per cent gradient produces something approaching a 50 per cent increase in calorie expenditure.

In particular, of course, the effect of your walking speed on energy expenditure is critical. The table shows the calorie costs of different walking speeds. These costs can be adjusted for body weight, for the steepness of the gradient and for the type of walking surface.

An output target of 200 to 400 Calories per session should be aimed at if a significant improvement in fitness and weight is to be obtained. Table 1 on the opposite page should help you establish the method most suitable for you.

186

TABLE 1 : VARIETIES OF WALKING AND ASSOCIATED CALORIE COSTS *

Walk	Speed		Calorie cost per hr.*	Comments
	m.p.h.	feet/sec.		
1. Amble	$1\frac{1}{2}$–2	2 –3	175	Barely faster than a queue shuffle. Long double stance phase, short swing phase.
2. Stroll	2 –$2\frac{1}{2}$	3 –$3\frac{1}{2}$	200	Casual walk; no arm swing is necessary.
3. Slow Walk	$2\frac{1}{2}$–3	$3\frac{1}{2}$–$4\frac{1}{2}$	240	The unhurried, quietly reflective walk of the preoccupied.
4. Easy Walk	3 –$3\frac{1}{2}$	$4\frac{1}{2}$–5	285	A comfortable walk that can be kept up all day.
5. Standard Walk	$3\frac{1}{2}$–4	5 –6	340	A purposeful walk that is about as fast as, or slightly faster than, the average pedestrian on a city street.
6. Brisk Walk	4 –$4\frac{1}{2}$	6 –$6\frac{1}{2}$	400	A brisk walk is defined as that walk which is fast enough to be so taxing that it cannot be maintained much longer than one hour.
7. Striding	$4\frac{1}{2}$–5	$6\frac{1}{2}$–$7\frac{1}{2}$	470	By lengthening the stride without losing the cadence of the brisk walk an increase of speed can be achieved.
8. Fast Walk	5 –$5\frac{1}{2}$	$7\frac{1}{2}$–8	555	To achieve a really fast walk the pelvis must be rotated forward with the leg as it swings through. The arms must also be swung, with elbows bent, like a runner.
9. Hard Walk	$5\frac{1}{2}$–6	8 –9	630	A hard walk is defined as that walk which cannot be maintained for more than about five minutes before exhaustion sets in.
10. Sprint Walk	6 –7	9 –10	720	Although race walking athletes can pound along for hours at speeds almost 50 per cent faster than this, you will be doing well to maintain this speed for more than a minute at a time.

* For a standard reference individual weighing 11 stone (154 lb., 70 kg.).

For convenience energy expenditures are expressed in Calories per hour but it is not anticipated that the higher energy cost activities will necessarily be maintained without pause for this length of time (see text).

A programme of walking is set out in Table 2. After week 20 the programme should remain relatively unchanged, but with minor modifications being introduced as appropriate to maintain a progressive and interesting schedule.

This programme may be interpreted best if an example is given. On Monday, Week 3, a varying pace workout is scheduled. This consists of an alternating series of Brisk and Standard walks each lasting five minutes repeated twice. That would take twenty minutes. The remaining five minutes of the session would be spent in warming up and tapering off.

The programme is only one of an almost infinite number of similar programmes that could have been presented and may not suit every individual. It can, however, be modified easily to meet a variety of needs in the following ways:

- The sessions may be lengthened or shortened, though a minimum of half an hour should be observed whenever possible.
- The type of workout may be altered — some people may prefer the rather gentle exercise of the even-paced sessions, while some may prefer the more vigorous and exhausting exercise provided by the Stop-Go workouts.
- Walking speed can be changed as needed, but the basic training stress should always exceed about 150 Calories per day for women and 200 Calories per day for men.

Running

The running schedule is the natural extension of the walking schedule over which it has one important advantage: it is more efficient. The calorie expenditure of moderate running is about twice that of moderate walking, so the time spent on an exercise session may be cut in half without loss in weight reduction.

At the simplest level, the running schedule requires that you run gently for about half an hour per day on three or four days each week. However, it is most effective when it leads you through a progressive programme similar to that for walking, outlined above. The calorie costs associated with varying degrees of activity are shown in Table 3. Individual weight must again be taken into consideration.

Because the calorie costs of running at all stages are much higher than those for comparable standards of walking, only a few overweight people will consider running long at those levels listed in the second half of the table. Fatigue develops quickly at the higher speeds, consequently the programme shown in Table 4 begins with quite short sessions of gentle running designed for the unfit. Over a period of twenty weeks, however, longer, more varied and harder workouts are progressively introduced.

As with the walking schedule, modifications may readily be introduced. For instance, you may wish to follow almost on a permanent basis the schedule outlined for the first six weeks only — you will still make progress if you vary your speed and the duration of the exercise. On the other hand, you may prefer to confine yourself to the sessions outlined for the later weeks of the programme.

TABLE 2: WALKING PROGRAMME FOR SLIMMERS*

| Week | Day | Min. | Type of Workout | The High Intensity Phase | |
| | | | | Main Level | Secondary Level |
				Style (Repetitions × Minutes)	Style (Repetitions × Minutes)
1	Mon	5	EVEN PACE	Standard (1×5)	—
	Wed	10	EVEN PACE	Standard (1×10)	—
	Fri	15	EVEN PACE	Standard (1×15)	—
2	Mon	20	EVEN PACE	Striding (1×20)	—
	Wed	20	EVEN PACE	Striding (1×20)	—
	Fri	20	EVEN PACE	Striding (1×20)	—
3	Mon	25	VARYING PACE	Brisk (2×5)	Standard (2×5)
	Wed	30	VARYING PACE	Brisk (2×5)	Standard (3×5)
	Fri	35	VARYING PACE	Brisk (3×5)	Standard (3×5)
4	Mon	25	EVEN PACE	Brisk (1×15)	—
	Wed	30	EVEN PACE	Brisk (1×20)	—
	Fri	35	EVEN PACE	Brisk (1×25)	—
5	Mon	35	VARYING PACE	Fast (2×5)	Standard (2×10)
	Wed	45	VARYING PACE	Fast (2×5)	Standard (3×10)
	Fri	50	VARYING PACE	Fast (3×5)	Standard (3×10)
6	Mon	30	EVEN PACE	Brisk (1×30)	—
	Wed	35	EVEN PACE	Brisk (1×35)	—
	Fri	40	EVEN PACE	Brisk (1×40)	—
7–8	Mon	40	STOP-GO	Hard (10×1)	Two-minute rests
	Wed	45	VARYING PACE	Fast (3×5)	Striding (4×5)
	Fri	40	STOP-GO	Hard (10×1)	Two-minute rests
9–10	Mon	45	EVEN PACE	Brisk (1×45)	—
	Wed	45	VARYING PACE	Fast (3×5)	Striding (4×5)
	Fri	40	STOP-GO	Hard (10×1)	Two-minute rests
11–15	Mon	20	EVEN PACE	Fast (1×20)	—
	Wed	45	VARYING PACE	Fast (3×5)	Striding (4×5)
	Fri	40	STOP-GO	Hard (10×1)	One-minute rests
16–20	Mon	20	EVEN PACE	Fast (1×20)	—
	Wed	45	VARYING PACE	Hard (7×1)	Standard (6×5)
	Fri	45	STOP-GO	Sprint (12×$\frac{1}{2}$)	Two-minute rests

* In all except the EVEN PACE sessions a warm-up period should precede the workout. This warm-up should be longer for the STOP-GO than for the VARYING PACE sessions and may be as long as fifteen minutes. Following each session a short period of gentle exercise should be allowed as a tapering-off period; the more intensive the workout the longer the tapering-off period. The difference between the stated session duration and the duration of the main workout is made up in each case by the warm-up and taper-off periods.

TABLE 3: VARIETIES OF RUNNING AND ASSOCIATED CALORIE COSTS

Style of Run*	Speed		Calorie cost per hr.	Comments
	m.p.h.	feet/sec.		
1. Shack	3–4	4–6	380	A slow, loose-limbed, flat-footed jog.
2. Jog	4–5	6–7	485	A somewhat bouncy but relaxed run, with a rather short stride length.
3. Slow Run	5–6	7–9	590	Less bouncy than the jog, longer stride but a slower cadence.
4. Easy Run	6–7	9–10	695	Easiest, most comfortable speed that you feel you could keep up almost indefinitely.
5. Standard Run	7–8	10–12	800	A modest paced run that you feel taxes your energy reserves and that you could not keep up for more than about a half to one hour.
6. Striding	8–9	12–13	905	By lengthening your stride without altering the cadence of the standard run you will run into exhaustion in about fifteen minutes.
7. Fast Run	9–10	13–15	1010	The fast run requires real effort and builds up an exhausted state within five minutes.
8. Hard Run	10–11	15–16	1120	All runs may seem hard, but for any one individual a hard run is defined as that run which cannot be continued for more than about 30 seconds.
9. Sprint	11 plus	16 plus	1300 plus	The maximum speed of which you are capable over about 30–60 yards.

* The 'style' of run is determined primarily by the *effort* put into the run by the individual who is running, for what might be an 'easy' run for one person may, of course, be a very hard run indeed for another. The speeds that are listed in association with each style are, therefore, merely an illustration of the kind of change of speed which will normally occur with each change of effort. Athletes may, for instance, decide that a 2 m.p.h. step is appropriate to their level of fitness while the overweight office worker may feel unable to face increments greater than $\frac{1}{2}$ m.p.h.

TABLE 4: RUNNING PROGRAMME FOR SLIMMERS*

| | | | | The High Intensity Phase | |
| | | | | Main Level | Secondary Level |
Week	Day	Min.	Type of Workout	Style (Repetitions × Minutes)	Style (Repetitions × Minutes)
1	*Mon	5	EVEN PACE	Shack (1×5)	—
	*Wed	10	EVEN PACE	Jog (1×10)	—
	*Fri	15	EVEN PACE	Jog (1×15)	—
2	Mon	20	EVEN PACE	Slow (1×20)	—
	Wed	20	EVEN PACE	Slow (1×20)	—
	Fri	20	EVEN PACE	Slow (1×20)	—
3	Mon	15	VARYING PACE	Easy (1×5)	Slow (1×5)
	Wed	20	VARYING PACE	Easy (1×5)	Slow (2×5)
	Fri	25	VARYING PACE	Easy (2×5)	Slow (2×5)
4	Mon	15	EVEN PACE	Easy (1×15)	—
	Wed	15	EVEN PACE	Easy (1×15)	—
	Fri	15	EVEN PACE	Easy (1×15)	—
5	Mon	20	VARYING PACE	Standard (1×5)	Slow (1×5)
	Wed	15	EVEN PACE	Easy (1×15)	—
	Fri	20	EVEN PACE	Easy (1×20)	—
6	Mon	25	VARYING PACE	Standard (2×5)	Slow (1×5)
	Wed	30	VARYING PACE	Standard (2×5)	Slow (2×5)
	Fri	15	EVEN PACE	Standard (1×15)	—
7–8	Mon	20	EVEN PACE	Standard (1×20)	—
	Wed	35	STOP-GO	Fast (6×$\frac{1}{2}$)	Two-minute rests
	Fri	20	EVEN PACE	Standard (1×20)	—
9–10	Mon	40	VARYING PACE	Brisk (3×5)	Slow (3×5)
	Wed	30	STOP-GO	Fast (8×$\frac{1}{2}$)	Two-minute rests
	Fri	40	VARYING PACE	Brisk (3×5)	Slow (3×5)
11–15	Mon	25	EVEN PACE	Standard (1×25)	—
	Wed	40	VARYING PACE	Brisk (3×5)	Standard (3×5)
	Fri	30	STOP-GO	Fast (8×$\frac{1}{2}$)	One-minute rests
15–20	Mon	30	EVEN PACE	Standard (1×30)	—
	Wed	40	VARYING PACE	Striding (2×5)	Standard (3×5)
	Fri	45	STOP-GO	Fast (10×$\frac{1}{2}$)	One-minute rests

* If you are very unfit extend this first week's programme over two to three weeks to avoid injury or extreme discomfort.

Home and Office Exercises

The Value of Exercises
The dance or gymnastic type of exercises with which most people are familiar are less effective as slimming activities than those previously described, but they have two particular advantages. They are convenient, because they can be done with a minimum of fuss in the privacy of one's home. And they are specific, that is, they can strengthen and trim up particular muscles (e.g. abdominals) that are most in need of attention.

The Design of the Exercise Schedules
These programmes are designed around facilities that are generally available in the home or office.

There are eight exercises in each programme. Emphasis is laid upon abdominal exercises for obvious reasons, but also included are exercises for the back, arms and legs. A general conditioning effect is obtained by running through the full programme continuously without pause.

The summary pages are presented at the beginning of each programme for ready reference. The sets of repetitions range from the relatively easy (series A) to the relatively difficult (series E). You should start to feel the pressure of the exercises after two weeks. Continue to increase the work load over the next eight or ten weeks, progressing throughout the different levels of repetitions until you reach the series which best suits your abilities and which you can reasonably expect to stick to permanently.

Organisation
About three or four half-hourly exercise sessions should be planned each week. The schedule should be intensified a little each month.

Plan your exercises for those times of the day when you are normally least tired, best organised and least concerned with other matters, e.g. after the family have been despatched to work or to school – before they are up, or during the lunch hour. Fixing a time and advertising your intention will help establish a habit you will hesitate to neglect.

It is worthwhile, though not essential, to change into minimal light clothing. Underwear will do if you have no more appropriate kit. Light clothing allows a freedom of movement which you can enjoy, while at the same time it creates a businesslike attitude that can help you attack your exercises wholeheartedly and energetically.

Plan to have a bath after exercising if at all possible. It is relaxing and refreshing and will help you to recover your composure after an energetic workout.

How to begin
Read the detailed instructions for each exercise carefully before trying it out. Have a member of your family, or a friend, check your performance, then practise the exercise carefully until you are doing it correctly.

Do not try to work too hard during the first one or two sessions, but aim rather to achieve a good quality of performance, and a smooth changeover from one exercise to the next. When you have become familiar with the full schedule and your standard of performance is stylish then you can begin to increase the work load.

After about two weeks you should just be starting to feel the pressure of the exercises. Continue increasing the work load over the next eight to ten weeks until you have established the level of training that you can handle on a permanent basis.

The programmes are designed as follows:

- Programme I is designed for the bedroom,
- Programme II is designed for a bathroom of reasonable size, but may equally be used elsewhere,
- Programme III is designed for the lounge or office or wherever there is a carpeted floor,
- Programme IV is designed for the kitchen or office.

It doesn't really matter which programme you start with. Choose whichever is most convenient and appeals to you. When you have completed one programme to your satisfaction, you can choose another.

Programme I
Summary and Progression Chart

Name*	Illustration	Progression**				
		A	B	C	D	E
1. Leg Roll		5	10	15	20	30
2. Alternative Leg Tucking		4	8	12	24	50
3. Tattoo		3 sets	6 sets	9 sets	12 sets	15 sets
4. Quarter Sit Ups		10	20	30	40	50
5. Arm Circling		10	20	40	60	80

Name*	Illustration	Progression**				
		A	B	C	D	E
6. Half Squats		5	10	20	30	40
7. High Kicks		20	40	60	80	100
8. Spot Running		1 min.	2 min.	3 min.	4 min.	5 min.

* For a detailed description see the next few pages.

** Start your schedule using the number of repetitions listed under Series A. After two weeks' progress to repetition series B. Subsequently progress to series C in four weeks, to series D in eight weeks and to series E after four months.

Modify this rate of progression according to your ability. In particular accelerate through these stages in any exercise that you find easy.

194

Programme I
Description of Exercises

Name of Exercise	Description	Type of Exercise
1. *Leg Roll*	**Starting Position** Flat on your back on a bed or on the floor. Arms spread sideways, or holding firmly to a support. Raise both legs into the air until the thighs are vertical, keeping the legs either (a) flexed at the knee, or (b) straight. **Movement** Roll your legs down sideways to touch the bed or floor at your left side, then, without pausing, raise them up again, carry them over and lower them down at the other side. Repeat this movement rhythmically and steadily.	Oblique Abdominal
2. *Alternative Leg Tucking*	**Starting Position** Flat on your back in bed or on the floor. Arms at your side. **Movement** Take a deep breath, then raise one knee up to your chin. Use your arms to pull it in to you tightly. Exhale. Then, slowly, in time with your breathing, exchange legs. Continue without pause.	Abdominal

Name of Exercise	Description	Type of Exercise
3. Tattoo	**Starting Position** Flat on your back in bed, or on the floor, hands by your sides for support. Place a pillow in the small of your back if required. **Movement** Raise both legs, then beat a tattoo of twelve beats with your heels, six beats as you breathe in, and six as you breathe out. Repeat continuously. 	Abdominal and thigh
4. Quarter Sit Ups	**Starting Position** Flat on your back in bed, or on the floor, hands on your thighs. Cushion or pillow in the small of your back if required. **Movement** Slide your hands down your thighs until they reach your kneecaps, raising your head and shoulders just sufficiently for this to be done. Return to the starting position quickly and, without pausing, bounce back up again to touch your kneecaps once more. Repeat continuously. 	Abdominal

Name of Exercise	Description	Type of Exercise
5. *Arm Circling*	**Starting Position** Sitting on the edge of the bed or chair arms raised sideways to shoulder height, palms facing downwards. **Movement** Circle your arms in small slow circles pressing them strongly backwards, down, then forwards and up. The entire circling movement should be out of the line of sight of your eyes. 	Arm and Shoulder
6. *Half Squats*	**Starting Position** Standing, back to bed or chair, with one foot in advance of the other. Arms folded. **Movement** Quickly but gently squat to touch the bed or chair with your seat, then immediately stand up again to your full height. Without pause repeat continuously. 	Leg

197

Name of Exercise	Description	Type of Exercise
7. *High Kicks*	**Starting Position** Standing, arms spread sideways for balance, and feet together. **Movement** Jump lightly a few inches into the air then on landing begin to kick first one and then the other leg high into the air in front of you, bouncing rhythmically in time with your kicking. Bounce once as your kicking foot reaches its highest point and once as it returns to the ground. Continue rhythmically.	Leg and abdominal

Name of Exercise	Description	Type of Exercise
8. Spot Running	**Starting Position** Standing, looking at any convenient mark that is about 4 in. above eye level. **Movement** Run on the spot, bouncing up on each pace to bring your eyes level with the selected marker.	Leg and general

Programme II
Summary and Progression Chart

Name	Illustration	Progression				
		A	B	C	D	E
1. Shoulder Stretching		10	10	10	10	10
2. Arm Swinging		10	15	20	25	30
3. Leg Changing		20	40	60	80	100
4. Pelvic Twist and Tilt		3	6	9	12	15

Name	Illustration	Progression				
		A	B	C	D	E
5. Cross Over Leg Swinging		5	10	15	20	25
6. Humping and Hollowing		20	30	40	50	60
7. Deep Knee Bending		5	10	15	20	30
8. Skip Jumping		1 min.	2 min.	3 min.	4 min.	5 min.

Programme II
Description of Exercises

Name of Exercise	Description	Type of Exercise
1. *Shoulder Stretching*	**Starting Position** Standing at the open window, feet apart **Movement** Breathe in steadily raising your arms to shoulder height as you do so, then press steadily backwards with your arms still at shoulder height to open up your chest fully. Press five times in this position rhythmically. Then exhale and lower your arms to your sides. Repeat. 	Preparatory and thoracic
2. *Arm Swinging*	**Starting Position** Standing with feet about six inches astride, arms raised forward to shoulder height. **Movement** Let your arms drop to swing downwards and backwards. As they reach the limit of their backwards swing rise up on your toes. As the arms swing down on their return movement, bend at the knees and hips then straighten up and rise on your toes as your arms reach their maximum forward height. Repeat continuously and rhythmically.	Arm and Trunk

(see diagram p. 204)

Name of Exercise	Description	Type of Exercise
3. Leg Changing	**Starting Position** Arms straight, hands resting on, say, the side of a bath, supporting your inclined body. **Movement** Lift one knee up to your chest, then with a slight jump change knees. Continue rhythmically without pause.	Leg, abdominal and general

Name of Exercise	Description	Type of Exercise
4. *Pelvic Twist and Tilt*	**Starting Position** Standing, feet slightly apart, arms raised sideways for balance, eyes fixed forwards on a convenient marker at eye level. **Movement** Without altering the position of head or feet, twist your hips rhythmically first to the left and then to the right. Repeat ten times. Then, with your weight on your straight left leg, drop your right hip down as far as it will go letting your right leg bend as you drop, then raise it up as high as you can. Repeat this five times, standing on the left leg, and five times standing on the right. Repeat the entire series as frequently as specified.	Waist
5. *Cross over Leg Swing-ing*	**Starting Position** Arms straight, hands resting on the side of the bath, trunk horizontal, feet together. **Movement** Carry the left leg across the body and raise it up to the right as far as it will go. Then swing it down again and up to the left. Continue this alternate swinging from left to right rhythmically, working hard to carry the leg higher at the limits of each excursion. Change to the right leg and repeat.	Abdominal and Leg *(see diagram p. 206)*

205

Name of Exercise	Description	Type of Exercise

6. *Humping and Hollowing*	**Starting Position** Standing, bending forward at the waist with hands on the edge of bath. **Movement** Stretch your arms and raise your hips and back as high as you can, tightening up abdominals to help. Then sag as deeply as you can lowering your chest and abdomen, and bending your arms as much as you can. Repeat slowly, breathing in regularly.	Back, Arm and Abdominal

 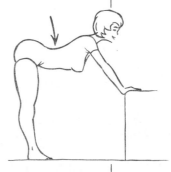

Name of Exercise	Description	Type of Exercise
7. *Deep Knee Bending*	**Starting Position** Standing, holding the bath side. **Movement** Rise on your toes, then bend your knees, and lower down into a full crouch position, keeping your back straight. Bounce gently once and then stand up again. Continue without pause.	Leg

Name of Exercise	Description	Type of Exercise
8. *Skip Jumping*	**Starting Position** Standing, eyes fixed on a marker about four inches above eye level. **Movement** Jump up in the air to bring your eyes level with the marker. Repeat the jump continuously without pause, bouncing up from the ground lightly each time. 	Leg and general

Programme III
Summary and Progression Chart

Name	Illustration	Progression				
		A	B	C	D	E
1. Kneeling, Tuck and Stretch		4	8	12	16	20
2. Back Raising		10	15	20	25	30
3. Sitting Twists		5	10	15	20	25
4. Leg Raising		5	10	15	20	25

Name	Illustration	Progression				
		A	B	C	D	E
5. Side Arching		5 sets	10 sets	15 sets	20 sets	25 sets
6. Press Ups		2	4	6	8	10
7. Squat Thrusts		10	20	30	40	50
8. Hopping		10 sets	20 sets	30 sets	40 sets	50 sets

Programme III
Description of Exercises

Name of Exercise	Description	Type of Exercise
1. *Kneeling, Tuck and Stretch*	**Starting Position** On hands and knees. **Movement** Raise one knee up to your chest and bend your head and chest over it. Then push the leg out behind you, lift it high and arch your back. Breathe out slowly as you bend your knee up and breathe in as you stretch it out. Continue slowly and rhythmically with alternate legs.	Preparatory and Back
2. *Back Raising*	**Starting Position** Flat on your face, hands clasped behind your back. **Movement** Raise your head, and legs away from the floor. Breathe in. Hold briefly, then lower. Exhale. Continue steadily.	Back

Name of Exercise	Description	Type of Exercise
3. *Sitting Twists*	**Starting Position** Sitting, legs straight and wide apart, both arms to the right side. **Movement** Turn to the left and touch both hands to the floor behind your back, then twist round to the opposite side and repeat. Continue slowly exerting effort to turn further in the limiting positions. 	Oblique Abdominal
4. *Leg Raising*	**Starting Position** Flat on your back, arms overhead holding on to some support. **Movement** Raise both legs up and over your head to touch your hands then lower back to the floor. Keep your legs straight throughout if you can, but bend them if necessary. Repeat steadily and continuously. 	Abdominal

Name of Exercise	Description	Type of Exercise
5. *Side Arching*	**Starting Position** Sitting on your left side, legs straight along the floor, one foot slightly in advance of the other, supporting yourself on your left arm. Keep your right arm at your side. **Movement** Raise your hips from the floor and arch them sideways high into the air supporting your weight on your left arm and both feet. Lower and repeat 10 times to the left and 10 times to the right for one complete set.	Lateral trunk

Name of Exercise	Description	Type of Exercise
6. *Press Ups or Kneeling Press Ups*	**Starting Position** On hands and knees, arms straight and thighs vertical. **Movement** **Either** (a) Bend your arms to bring your chin down to touch the floor, then press up again until your arms are straight. **Or,** if you are strong enough (b) Raise your knees clear of the ground, to support your weight on only your hands and feet, before bending your arms to bring your chin to the floor. Repeat steadily. 	Arm

Name of Exercise	Description	Type of Exercise
7. *Squat Thrusts*	**Starting Position** Crouching down with hands on the floor, and knees between arms. **Movement** Jump your feet back as far as you can without losing your balance, then immediately bounce back again into the crouch position. Without pause repeat rhythmically.	Trunk

Name of Exercise	Description	Type of Exercise
8. *Alternate Leg Hopping*	**Starting Position** Standing on the left leg, holding the right leg in the left hand. Eyes should be looking at a marker about four inches above eye level. Movement Hop up until the eyes are level with the marker ten times then change legs. Ten hops on each leg constitutes one set.	Leg and General

Programme IV
Summary and Progression Chart

Name	Illustration	Progression				
		A	B	C	D	E
1. Corner Stretching		10	10	10	10	10
2. Double Tattoo		3	6	9	12	15
3. Buttock Lifting		5	10	15	20	30
4. Bob and Twist		20	40	60	80	100

Name	Illustration	Progression				
		A	B	C	D	E
5. Bow and Bend		5	10	15	20	30
6. Table Push Ups		3	6	9	12	15
7. Door Jumping		5	10	20	30	40
8. High Knee Raising		20	40	80	160	320

Programme IV
Description of Exercises

Name of Exercise	Description	Type of Exercise
1. *Corner Stretching*	**Starting Position** Standing, facing into a corner, with one foot slightly in advance of the other, arms raised above shoulder height, and hands resting on the corner walls. **Movement** Using the walls to force back your arms arch your back, transfer your weight on to your front foot and press your chest into the corner, stretching your shoulders and spine as fully as you can. After a brief pause step back into the starting position, and repeat.	Preliminary Stretching

Name of Exercise	Description	Type of Exercise
2. *Double Tattoo*	**Starting Position** Sitting leaning backwards, holding on to the seat of a chair with both hands, legs stretched out in front of you. **Movement** Raise both feet quickly off the ground until they are horizontal, then drop them back again. Repeat continuously and vigorously without pausing. Keep your legs straight, or as straight as you can, throughout the movement. 	Abdominal
3. *Buttock Lifting*	**Starting Position** Sitting erect, arms folded. **Movement** Raise the right thigh and buttock sideways up in the direction of your right armpit. Arch your body sideways over the *raised* hip as you do so. Lower and repeat to the opposite side. 	Lateral Abdominal

Name of Exercise	Description	Type of Exercise
4. Bob and Twist	**Starting Position** Standing, feet a few inches apart, with your back to a table or desk, and your eyes fixed in front of you on some convenient marker. **Movement** Without taking your eyes off the marker, twist your body round and bend your knees until you can just touch the table top with both hands. As soon as you have done so, bob up again and twist to the opposite side. One movement is completed when you have bobbed and twisted, once to each side. Repeat continuously and rhythmically. 	Leg and Abdominal
5. Bow and Bend	**Starting Position** Standing, facing a table or desk, feet together, hands lightly touching the table top. **Movement** Bow from the waist until your nose lightly touches the table top then straighten up again. Immediately, while keeping your back erect, rise on your toes, then bend your legs and crouch down until your eyes are level with the table top. Stand up again, and lower your heels. Repeat this movement smoothly and continuously. *(see diagram p. 222)*	Back and Leg

221

Name of Exercise	Description	Type of Exercise

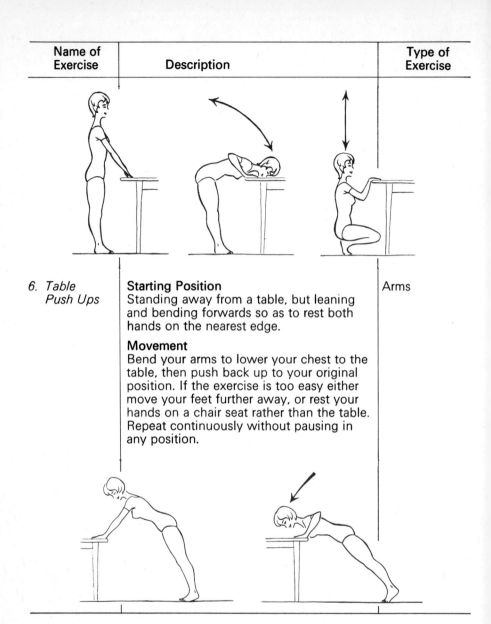

6. *Table Push Ups*	**Starting Position** Standing away from a table, but leaning and bending forwards so as to rest both hands on the nearest edge. **Movement** Bend your arms to lower your chest to the table, then push back up to your original position. If the exercise is too easy either move your feet further away, or rest your hands on a chair seat rather than the table. Repeat continuously without pausing in any position.	Arms

Name of Exercise	Description	Type of Exercise
7. *Door Jumping*	**Starting Position** Standing on tip-toe, arms raised to touch door jamb or wall above door, at full stretch height. Mentally note a mark about 4 in. above your finger tip height. **Movement** Jump up to touch the mark repeatedly without pause.	Leg and General

Name of Exercise	Description	Type of Exercise
8. High Knee Raising	**Starting Position** Standing, looking at any convenient marker that is about 4 in. above your eye level. **Movement** Run on the spot, raising your knees to waist height and bouncing up on each step to bring your eyes level with the selected mark. 	Leg and General

Sports Schedule for Slimmers

Even quite active individuals may find the idea of exercise for exercise's sake basically unattractive. They need the motivating interest or the excitement of games and sports to drive them to vigorous activity. For those who are of this turn of mind there are many alternative sports from which to choose. The final choice will inevitably be influenced by various factors specific to the individual, but since the result aimed at is increased slimness and fitness, you must participate in your chosen sport with the same intensity as you would embark on the formal exercise schedules.

The approximate energy costs of different sports is presented in Table 5. Check which calorie cost classification your sport falls under to judge how long you must play to achieve the 200–400 Calorie expenditure per day that is the appropriate training load for the would-be slimmer.

TABLE 5: ENERGY EXPENDITURE IN SPORTING ACTIVITIES

Type of Activity	Name of Sport	Classification of Calorie Costs*
1. *Marksmanship*	Billiards	Light
	Archery	Light
	Rifle Shooting	Light
	Bowls (Green)	Light
	Boule	Light
	Bowling (Ten Pin)	Light to Moderate
	Bowling (Cricket)	Moderate
	Croquet	Light
	Golf	Light
2. *Aesthetic*	Dance	Light to Moderate
	Gymnastics	Moderate
	Diving	Light to Moderate
	Trampolining	Moderate
3. *Racquet Games*	Table-Tennis	Light
	Tennis	Moderate
	Badminton	Light to Moderate
	Squash	Heavy
4. *Water Sports*	Sailing	Light
	Surfing/Skiing	Light to Moderate
	Canoeing	Light to Moderate
	Rowing	Light to Moderate
	Sub-aqua swimming	Moderate
	Swimming	Moderate to Heavy

Type of Activity	Name of Sport	Classification of Calorie Costs *
5. *Locomotor Sports*	Rambling	Moderate
	Orienteering	Moderate
	Climbing	Moderate to Heavy
	Skating	Moderate
	Skiing	Moderate to Heavy
	Cycling	Moderate
6. *Team Games*	Cricket	Light
	Volleyball	Light to Moderate
	Basketball	Moderate
	Softball/Baseball	Light to Moderate
	Hockey	Moderate
	Football	Moderate to Heavy
	Rugby	Heavy
	Water Polo	Heavy
	Lacrosse	Moderate
	Handball	Heavy
7. *Combat Sports*	Fencing	Moderate
	Judo	Moderate
	Karate	Moderate
	Wrestling	Heavy
	Boxing	Heavy

* Footnote

Energy Expenditure	Caiorie Costs per hour
Light	125–220
Light to Moderate	220–315
Moderate	315–395
Moderate to Heavy	395–475
Heavy	475–1,000 plus

In compiling the above regard has been paid not to the maximum Calorie costs that might be incurred by a well-trained and fit young person but to those probably reasonably achieved by only an averagely motivated one. The costs listed here are, therefore, much lower than are attainable.

In this chapter, a very simple message has been given. It boils down to this: if you want to lose weight in the quickest way, you must not only control your diet, but also increase your activity. Different ways of making this activity more interesting, safe and effective have been outlined.

CHAPTER TWELVE

Slimmers' Forum

THERE IS no doubt about it – slimming is not an easy business. This explains why so many people are always ready with excuses to explain why they cannot slim, and why so many people are always ready to clutch at any new method which offers them an apparently easy way to lose weight. In this section I have tried to deal with most of the excuses and the treatments and to sort out the truthful and doubtful elements of them both.

Is Fatness Inherited?

It is known that a child with one fat parent has a 50 per cent chance of becoming fat and that a child with two fat parents has a 70–80 per cent chance of becoming fat.

However, it is more or less impossible to distinguish between the genetically and socially inherited characteristics to which a growing child is subjected. If the parents are in the habit of eating large meals, it is quite likely that their children will also be made to overeat and therefore get fat.

In Britain, fat people are more likely to be found among the working classes, whereas in countries such as India the upper classes are fatter. This surely reflects the eating habits of the families concerned.

However, it is also possible that fat parents, or those who tend to become fat, do produce children with a similar tendency. Surveys of identical twins where one of the twins was brought up by another family have shown that both environmental and genetic influences play a part in the determining body weight. Another survey compared the weight of adopted children with the weight of natural children. There was much less correlation between the weights of the adopted children and their adoptive parents than between the natural children and their parents.

At the moment no one knows exactly what this inherited 'tendency towards fatness' is. Some of the most interesting recent research has shown that the actual number of fat cells that a young baby has is critical in deciding whether that baby is likely to become fat if he overeats. This is why it is so important to make sure that very young babies, especially those with fat parents, are not overfed.

Can 'Cellulite' Be My Trouble?

Cellulite is the term used on the Continent to describe a lumpy, knobbly sort of fat which gives the skin in certain 'cellulite' areas a dimpled appearance. Firms and salons who market 'Anti-cellulite' devices claim that this sort of fat will not disappear with dieting and therefore persuade people to buy various lotions, creams and massagers to apply to their 'cellulite' areas. There is no good evidence that massage or rubbing things into your skin can get rid of ordinary fat. Even if 'cellulite fat' is any different from ordinary fat – and this is a questionable matter – it is also extremely unlikely that self-massage will do any good at all. If you do have lumpy areas of fat which perhaps are more painful than other areas, it is best to see your doctor to see if there is anything he can do about it before you start self-medication.

Why does Dieting seem to have no Effect on the Fat in Certain Areas of My Body?

This question is often asked by women who are quite pleased with their general slimming success but still frustrated by what seems to be immovable lumps of fat usually on the lower half of their body. Unfortunately, the tendency to deposit fat and where it is deposited is probably dependent on genetic influences and general metabolism and is a long way from being fully understood. If you have a heavy bottom half one remedy is to cut down the time that you spend sitting down and try to move around more. Quite a number of women notice the difference when they give up a completely sedentary job for a less sedentary one. Apart from this, there is nothing that I can recommend.

How does My Weight Vary Normally?

Your weight can vary by a few pounds during the course of a day. This is why it is so important to weigh yourself at the same time each day. You will probably be at your lightest first thing in the morning – after you have emptied your bowels and bladder and before you have had breakfast.

Women usually have a monthly fluctuation in their weight. You will probably weigh your heaviest in the week before your period is due – perhaps 2 to 3 lb. more than normal. But do not worry, this is only because you retain more fluid than usual at this time – your weight will return to normal very soon after your period has started. If you do find that this happens, bear it in mind when you are slimming and do not be discouraged if you do not seem to be losing much weight in the week before your period is due. If you have a true calorie deficit you will still be losing *fat* even though your weight might not change much. You will probably find that you will lose more weight than normal in the week after your period has started.

Could the Pill make Me Fat?

Quite a number of women who start taking oral contraceptives find that their weight begins to creep up at the same time. This is probably because the two hormones in the Pill, oestrogen and progesterone, are altering the metabolism of the body. They might be causing more fluid retention than usual; in this case the increase in weight would be due to increased water. Or they might be causing you to store slightly more fat than usual. As yet, no large scale survey has thrown any light on this problem, although it has been suggested that up to half of the women on the Pill do suffer in this way. The unfortunate thing is that these tend to be the ones who have a natural weight problem anyway.

If you are one of these women, talk to your doctor about it and he will probably prescribe another brand of pill. Different brands contain the two hormones in different proportions and quite often an alternative brand will not affect your metabolism in this way.

Could Giving Up Smoking make Me Fat?

About one in ten of the slimmers taking part in a recent survey said that giving up smoking was one of the things that made them fat, and a large scale survey carried out among steel workers in South Wales showed that non-smokers and ex-smokers tended to be quite a lot heavier than smokers.

Whether smoking has any direct effect on metabolism (i.e. preventing fat formation) is not yet known, but there is strong evidence that a cigarette or pipe can be an effective appetite reducer. And, of course, there is the simple fact that you cannot eat when you are smoking.

Both smoking and obesity are serious health hazards, and there is clearly a need for studies to determine the relationship between the two hazards. All that can be said at present is that if you do give up smoking you should make a special effort to watch your weight. If you have to eat more sweets to stop putting a cigarette in your mouth, remember that these are usually quite high in calories and carbohydrate and that you should eat slightly less at meal times to compensate. Chewing unsweetened gum often helps smokers to break the habit without doing too much damage to their figure or their teeth.

What is Wrong with Crash Diets?

By a 'crash diet' I mean the sort of diet that you find in some newspapers and magazines which promises a 5 or 10 lb. weight loss in an equal number of days. If you stick rigidly to the diet, forcing yourself to eat the weird concoctions such as raw egg yolks, grapefruit and honey that are often advocated, you probably will lose the stated amount of weight (although a good proportion will be water only) and remain perfectly healthy. BUT, you will not learn much about nutrition or weight control; you will probably find it rather monotonous and you are quite likely to put back all the lost weight once you start eating normally again. Still, this is the method by which some people like to slim and so for them here is the simplest crash diet that I know: Drink no more than two pints of milk and take one vitamin pill every day. You can take the milk in unsweetened or artificially sweetened tea or coffee. This will give you less than 800 Calories a day and you should lose at least 3 lb. in the week. (Do not follow this diet for more than a week at a time.)

Can Heat Treatment Help?

Several slimming salons are now offering treatments whereby direct heat with electric bandages is applied to those parts of the body which are too fat. It is claimed that this heat treatment speeds up the work of the enzymes responsible for breaking down fat. Unfortunately, the enzymes of the human body are ingeniously designed to work best at normal body temperatures and so the best you can hope for from this treatment is a temporary loss of water.

Can Complete Meal Substitutes Help?

There are several different products sold for slimmers which can all be grouped together under the general heading of meal substitutes. They are really aids for slimmers who want to restrict what they eat but cannot be bothered with too much counting or the preparation of low calorie meals. By eating one of the recommended meals they can be sure of eating only the stated number of calories without depriving themselves of any essential nutrients.

You can buy a whole variety of these meals – chocolate biscuits, savoury sandwiches, chocolate bars, etc. Each packet tells you how many biscuits should be taken to make up a meal – usually about 300 Calories. Some products contain a bulking agent so that the meal will make you feel fuller than if you ate a normal meal without the bulking agent. They can be very useful in a situation where you want a quick low calorie snack and you really have not the time to prepare one yourself (say, for the office worker at lunchtime). An advantage is that you know exactly how many calories are in the snack and can plan the rest of your day around that. They should always be eaten as meal substitutes and never be eaten on top of a meal.

Can Appetite-reducing Pills Help?

First, it is important to distinguish between the different types of pill.

There are about twenty different brands of pill all claiming to help you overcome your hunger pains. These pills often contain some type of bulking agent, usually methyl cellulose. The theory is that when you take them, they swell up inside your stomach to kid your brain into thinking that you are full up so that it switches off your appetite. One brand contains liquid glucose. Eating this is supposed to immediately raise the level of sugar in your blood. The makers claim that the effect this has is to make you less hungry, again by deceiving that area of the brain which is responsible for controlling your appetite. Unfortunately, the independent tests which have been done on these products so far have not produced very encouraging results. The pills do not reduce hunger any more than dummy pills and the amount of swelling they produce is negligible anyway.

So, it really does seem that it is not worth buying these products. Of course, you may know someone who swears by them and tells you about the weight she has lost. But more often than not she will admit to following some diet at the same time and will find it difficult to say whether or not the pills reduced her appetite.

The other type of appetite-reducing pills can only be obtained on a doctor's prescription. The amphetamine-type drugs are supposed to curb your appetite by a direct action on the appetite centre of the brain. Very few doctors are prescribing them these days because they can become addictive and the BMA now operates a voluntary ban on their prescription. There are other non-amphetamine-type drugs (not included in the ban) which your doctor may prescribe for you (e.g. Ponderax, Tenuate Dospan and Apisate). A survey of slimmers who had tried these drugs showed that they were just as effective as the amphetamines and caused fewer side effects.

It will be up to your doctor to decide whether he should prescribe these drugs for you. Some will not prescribe them on any account, while some will only prescribe them for patients who are grossly overweight or patients who have got 'stuck' at a certain weight after a reasonable loss.

But remember that taking pills is no good at all if they do not do what they are supposed to – and that means making you eat less. Unfortunately, there is no pill around, as yet, which will allow you to eat as much as you like without getting fat. Until that time comes, why not see whether you can find other ways of reducing your appetite ? You might find it helpful to drink a glass of water or a cup of coffee before or with your meal. Or you could have a small starter about half an hour before you sit down to your main meal.

Can Steam and Sauna Baths Help?

Anything that makes you sweat will obviously cause you to lose some body *water*. But this is *not* body *fat*. Although you might weigh a couple of pounds lighter after a sauna bath, you will put it all back on again immediately you eat or drink anything. Similarly, garments which you wear to make you sweat are not going to do you a ha'porth of good in the real business of getting rid of fat. So, leave this method of quick, but temporary, weight reduction to the jockeys.

Would It Help to Join a Slimming Group?

Without a doubt, most people who regard themselves as slimming failures would probably say that their own lack of willpower was the main reason why they did not get slim. They often lose a certain amount of weight but are then too weak-willed to carry on as they must if they are to get slim once and for all. It is these people, in particular, who can be helped by the moral support of a slimming group.

There cannot be many areas in the country which still lack a slimming group or club. The national organisations such as Weight Watchers, Slimming Magazine Clubs and Silhouette Clubs are opening up new classes at a rapid rate. The best place to see an advertisement for your nearest club is the local paper, although it is quite possible that another slimming-conscious colleague will introduce you to a club.

What are the advantages of these clubs, and why their success? Whatever club you join, they will all emphasise the same basic principle that is stressed in the previous parts of this book, i.e. to lose weight, your energy intake must be less than your energy output. Their methods of making you reduce your energy input will vary – some will suggest cutting carbohydrates while others will suggest you cut calories. As has already been explained, these are different means to the same end. They all hold weekly meetings and usually operate the sort of system whereby you have to pay even for those meetings you do not attend. The great thing is that every week you will meet people with the same problem and get help and encouragement from your lecturer. Although she has usually overcome her own weight problem, she will be all too familiar with the trials and temptations that face a slimmer. The groups make a big thing of the competitive element of slimming. You will be given a weight which the group thinks you could reach and there will be some sort of reward when you reach it – although the greatest reward is naturally to be slim. Most of the groups now operate some system whereby those members who have got slim are still considered as members of the club. This is to help them maintain their slim weight and not slip back into their old habits again.

Are there any disadvantages to the group method of slimming? There is the cost element, of course. The average weekly fee is about 75p. There is also the fact that you have to find time to attend the meetings. You could get over this latter problem by joining one of the slimming groups where the only communication between you and the group is by letter (such as Weight Checkers International) but then you would lose the 'group' element and have to rely on the regular arrival of your check-up sheet to jog your slimming conscience. Remember too, the togetherness principle can work in smaller circles. If another member of your family is also overweight, think up some way of competing with each other – or have regular get-togethers with a few overweight friends and try to spur each other on in this way.

Can Massage Help?

Being massaged by a trained masseur can certainly be a pleasant and relaxing experience. But no amount of flesh pummelling can have any permanent effect on the fat underneath. When you store fat it is deposited in individual fat cells – a mass of these make up your adipose tissue. The only way the fat can be released again is by the combined action of enzyme and hormones. Simple physical rubbing of fatty areas cannot possibly cause fat release. If you try one of the massage or vibrating belts it might feel that they are rubbing away at the layers of fat, but, unfortunately, there is no good evidence that they can do this. The tests done by *Which?* and by *Slimming Magazine* on different types of massaging devices ended up with the conclusion that none of them produced any signifcant loss of fat or inches on the test subjects.

CHAPTER THIRTEEN

The End of the Road

ONCE YOU HAVE got slim, you can certainly congratulate yourself on your success. BUT do not fall into the trap of resting on your laurels and forgetting all about your weight again. If you were fat once, this almost certainly means that you have a tendency to get fat if, at any time, you eat more than you need. Just because you have got rid of one lot of surplus fat this does not mean that new fat will not come back if you overeat again. Maintaining weight is obviously much more pleasant than losing weight, but it still follows the same basic rules.

So, if you have been a 1,000 Calories a day person while you have been losing weight, you will probably find that you will be able to eat about 1,500 to 2,000 Calories a day to maintain your new weight. It is impossible to estimate more accurately because individuals show so much variation. All you can do is to carry on weighing yourself as you did before and remain generally aware of your calorie intake. If your weight is staying reasonably constant, you will know roughly how many calories a day you need for maintaining this. If your weight is still going down, you can eat a little more and still be all right. However, if it starts to go up steadily, you have overestimated and you will have to cut down. As with losing weight, you should not worry about exceeding your limit on one day so long as you can make up for it beforehand or afterwards.

Those of you who decided to be carbohydrate cutters can alter your diet in two ways when you reach your target weight. If you find that you have lost your sweet tooth completely by restricting sugary and starchy things while you have been losing weight, you probably will not want to include them in your diet again and you will be able to eat more of the carbohydrate-free foods. If, however, you still have a craving for something sweet, you can let yourself have the occasional treat without it harming your weight. Again, you too must keep a very careful check on your weight and act quickly as soon as you see it taking an upward trend. If you look after the pounds, the stones will look after themselves.

The Ten Commandments of Slimming

1. To lose weight, you must take in fewer calories in the form of food and drink than you are using up for energy.
2. Carbohydrate cutting is an indirect method of calorie cutting. All foods, carbohydrate, fat and protein, are potential fat.
3. There are extremely few real excuses for fatness. Unfortunately, some people seem to have a greater 'tendency' towards fatness than others and they have to control their eating habits very carefully.
4. Slimming should be a gradual process. You should resign yourself to this fact and not expect miracles.
5. A lot of the machines and garments which are advertised as aids to slimming are rubbish and a waste of money. The best exercise is regular walking.
6. There are no magical 'slimming' foods but some calorie-reduced foods can be extremely useful to slimmers.
7. The way that foods are cooked can drastically alter their fattening potential. Stick to simple methods and avoid those using a lot of fat.
8. Once you have got slim, never forget what you have learnt and keep a watchful eye on your weight at all times.
9. Prevention is better than cure. Do not let babies and children get fat and you will probably save them having to slim later in life.
10. FINALLY, slimming *is* worth it. Persevere and you will find out for yourself.

Appendix A

Recipes by calorie content per portion

Recipes under 100 Calories

	Calories	CH Units	Page
Stuffings			
Lemon	65	2	73
Mushroom, tomato and celery	60	2¼	72
Packeted	35	1½	72
Rice and Liver	40	1	73
Fish and Shellfish Dishes			
Crabmeat stuffed tomatoes	65	1½	89
Shellfish cocktails, various	60-65	¾	89
Shrimp stuffed courgettes	55	0	88
Shrimp stuffed peppers	85	0	89
Shrimp stuffed tomatoes	75	1½	88
Smoked haddock mousse	90	0	84
White haddock mousse	90	0	84
Egg Dishes			
Egg, baked	90-100	0	97
boiled	70-90	0	92
poached	70-90	0	92
Salads			
Coleslaw	45	1½	125
Continental cucumber	10	0	126
Cucumber misère	15	0	126
Hot pepper salad	60	½	128
Jamaican savoury salad	75	2½	129
Orange and cauliflower salad	55	3¼	128
Oriental orange salad	60	3	127
Salad Niçoise	90	½	125
Salad Dressings			
Cottage cheese dressing	15	0	130
Slimmers' French dressing	45	0	130
Tomato juice dressing	15	0	132
Yoghurt salad dressing	20	¼	132

	Calories	CH Units	Page
Gravies and Sauces			
Pepper and tomato sauce	30	½	137
Slimmers' egg sauce	75	¾	136
Slimmers' savoury sauce	70	1¾	134
Slimmers' white sauce, coating	70	2½	134
Slimmers' white sauce, pouring	60	2	134
Yoghurt and mint sauce	20	¼	137
Desserts			
Baked fruit	50	2¼	150
Fresh fruit salad	65	3¼	145
Fruit fool (depending on fruit)	50-65	1½-2¼	148
Fruit jelly—Method 2	25-30	¾-1¼	152
Fruit mousse (depending on fruit)	35-55	1-2	148
Fruit sorbet (depending on fruit)	35-55	1-2	149
Slimmers' custard	70	2½	157

Recipes between 100-199 Calories

	Calories	CH Units	Page
Meat, Poultry and Offal Dishes			
Basic meat mould, chicken	165	½	70
Basic meat mould, pork	165	½	70
Basic meat mould, veal	165	½	70
Basic risotto, chicken	185	5	68
Basic risotto, pork	185	5	68
Basic risotto, veal	185	5	68
Chicken, roast	140	0	56
Liver, grilled	170	0	62
Pork chop lean, grilled	140	0	52
Pork, roast	140	0	56
Turkey, roast	140	0	56
Veal, grilled	140	0	52
Veal, roast	140	0	56
Stuffings			
Chestnut	195	7	74
Corn and onion	110	4¾	73
Fish and Shellfish Dishes			
Baked cod fillet	105	1½	87
Fish casserole	145	1	81
Fish cutlets in a foil parcel	160	½	77
Fish fillets in a foil parcel	150	0	78
Fish in cider	170	2½	81
Fish in wine	190	3½	81
Fruity baked fish	160	2½	77
Fruity fillets	195	4	79
Spicy mackerel (1)	130	½	85
Spicy mackerel (2)	125	¼	85

	Calories	CH Units	Page
Poached fish	125	¼	82
Salmon mousse	160	0	84
Smoked haddock in savoury sauce	145	1	86
Sweet and sour baked fish	160	½	77
Trout, grilled	150	0	80

Egg Dishes

Egg, fried	145	0	92
Egg, scrambled	120	0	93
Eggs in a bed of mushrooms and celery	100	0	97
Eggs in a bed of seafood	180	½	98
Eggs in a bed of spinach	110	0	97
Stuffed eggs with mushrooms	190	0	99
Tomato scramble	135	1	100

Cheese Dishes

Tasty cheese snack	130	0	105
Tomato and cheese casserole	185	1	105

Vegetable Dishes

Vegetables, stuffed (depends on vegetable and stuffing used)	Approx. 100-200	1-3	112
Vegetables with hardboiled egg	125	1¼	120

Desserts

Basic egg custard	115	1¼	157
Basic sweet soufflé omelette	195	0	154
Fruit cream (depending on fruit used)	110-130	1-2	149
Fruit jelly—Method 1	125	5½	152
Fruit mould (depending on fruit used)	100-120	1¾-2¾	153

Recipes between 200 and 299 Calories

Meat, Poultry and Offal Dishes

Basic meat loaf, chicken	215	½	67
Basic meat loaf, pork	215	½	67
Basic meat loaf, veal	215	½	67
Basic risotto, beef	265	5	68
Basic risotto, lamb	265	5	68
Basic slimmers' cottage pie, chicken	240	¾	69
Basic slimmers' cottage pie, pork	240	¾	69
Basic slimmers' cottage pie, veal	240	¾	69
Duck, roast	280	0	86
Kidneys in oxtail sauce	250	2¾	64
Liver casserole	215	2¼	63
Liver parcels	275	1¾	62
Pork with apple and cider	295	5	49
Slimmers' goulash, veal	240	2	49
Sweet and sour pork	250	2	48

	Calories	CH Units	Page
Stuffing	205	2	74
Sausage and celery			
Fish Dishes	250	3¼	76
Baked fish with egg sauce	280	¾	76
Baked herrings with vinegar sauce	210	1½	82
Poached fish au gratin			
Egg Dishes	200	0	98
Eggs in a bed of chicken livers	210	0	93
Omelette, basic	255	3¼	96
Soufflé, basic			
Cheese Dishes	210	3½	101
Cauliflower cheese	210	3	110
Cheese and banana salad	260	3	109
Cheese and cabbage casserole	280	3	111
Cheese puffs	285	0	103
Cheese stuffed peppers	235	0	104
Eggs and cheese en cocotte	295	0	109
French bean and cheese salad	280	3½	101
Slimmers' macaroni cheese.	255	1½	111
Slimmers' quiche			
Vegetable Dishes	265	4	121
Basic vegetable casserole	235	3	121
Tomato casserole	285	4	116
Vegetables au gratin	240	5	121
Vegetables in wine	225	3¾	119
Vegetables with poached egg	275	1	119
Vegetables with scrambled egg			
Salads	215	4¼	129
Egg and potato salad			
Desserts	255	3¼	156
Basic hot sweet soufflé			

300-399 Calories

Meat, Poultry and Offal Dishes			
Basic chicken casserole	345	¾	60
Basic meatburgers, beef	385	½	68
Basic meat loaf, beef	375	½	67
Basic meat loaf, lamb	375	½	67
Basic meat mould, beef	330	½	70
Basic meat mould, lamb	330	½	70
Beef, grilled	300	0	52
Beef, roast	300	0	56
Chicken and tomato casserole	360	1½	60

	Calories	CH Units	Page
Chicken curry	345	¾	61
Gammon, grilled	360	0	52
Lamb and kidney casserole	355	2	49
Lamb chop, lean grilled	300	0	52
Lamb kebabs	390	2¾	53
Lamb, roast	300	0	56
Mexican chicken	355	¾	60
Slimmers' savoury mince	300	1½	50
Tripe and onions	335	4	65
Veal fricassée	310	4½	51

Fish Dishes

	Calories	CH Units	Page
Baked stuffed fish	340	2½	79
Cheesey baked fish	325	3¼	76
Herrings, grilled	390	0	80
Smoked haddock omelette	380	0	87

Egg Dishes

	Calories	CH Units	Page
Floating islands	300	0	99

Cheese Dishes

	Calories	CH Units	Page
Cheese and chive scramble	365	0	103
Cheesey roes	360	3¼	108
Slimmers' cheese pie	320	1¾	104

400-499 Calories

Meat, Poultry and Offal Dishes

	Calories	CH Units	Page
Basic meat casserole	400	2	48
Basic slimmers' cottage pie, beef	405	¾	69
Basic slimmers' cottage pie, lamb	405	¾	69
Bolognese	400	6	51
Coq au vin	425	5½	61
Curried beef casserole	400	2	49
Duck à l'orange	445	5	61
Goulash, beef	400	2	49
Lamb stew	450	4	49
Oxtail stew	425	1¾	64
Polish slimmers' tripe	400	4	66
Sausage, grilled	400	4	52

Cheese Dishes

	Calories	CH Units	Page
Spanish cheese	465	1½	108

500 Calories and over

Meat, Poultry and Offal Dishes

	Calories	CH Units	Page
Lamb chop, lean and fat, grilled	600	0	52
Pork chop, lean and fat, grilled	520	0	52

Appendix B

Recipes by carbohydrate content per portion

Recipes containing no carbohydrates	*CH Units*	*Calories*	*Page*
Meat, Poultry and Offal Dishes			
Beef, grilled	0	300	52
Beef, roast	0	300	56
Chicken, roast	0	300	56
Duck, roast	0	280	56
Gammon, grilled	0	360	52
Lamb chop, lean and fat, grilled	0	600	52
Lamb chop, lean, grilled	0	300	52
Lamb, roast	0	300	56
Liver, grilled	0	170	62
Pork chop, lean and fat, grilled	0	520	52
Pork chop, lean, grilled	0	140	52
Pork, roast	0	140	56
Turkey, roast	0	140	56
Veal, grilled	0	140	52
Veal, roast	0	140	56
Fish and Shellfish Dishes			
Fish fillets in a foil parcel	0	150	78
Herrings, grilled	0	390	80
Salmon mousse	0	160	84
Shrimp stuffed courgettes	0	55	88
Shrimp stuffed peppers	0	85	89
Smoked haddock mousse	0	90	84
Smoked haddock omelette	0	380	87
Trout, grilled	0	150	80
White haddock mousse	0	90	84
Egg Dishes			
Egg, baked	0	90-100	97
boiled	0	70-90	92
fried	0	145	92
poached	0	70-90	92
scrambled	0	120	93
Eggs in a bed of chicken livers	0	200	98

	CH Units	Calories	Page
Eggs in a bed of mushrooms and celery	0	100	97
Eggs in a bed of spinach	0	110	97
Floating islands	0	300	99
Omelette, basic	0	210	93
Stuffed eggs with mushrooms	0	190	99

Cheese Dishes
Cheese and chive scramble	0	365	103
Cheese stuffed peppers	0	285	103
Eggs and cheese en cocotte	0	235	104
French bean and cheese salad	0	295	109
Tasty cheese snack	0	130	105

Salads
Continental cucumber	0	10	126
Cucumber misère	0	15	126

Salad Dressings
Cottage cheese dressing	0	15	130
Slimmers' French dressing	0	45	130
Tomato juice dressing	0	15	132
Yoghurt salad dressing	¼	20	132

Desserts
Basic sweet soufflé omelette	0	195	154

Less than 1 CH Unit

Meat, Poultry and Offal Dishes
Basic chicken casserole	¾	345	60
Basic meatburgers, beef	½	385	68
Basic meat loaf, beef	½	375	67
Basic meat loaf, chicken	½	215	67
Basic meat loaf, lamb	½	375	67
Basic meat loaf, pork	½	215	67
Basic meat loaf, veal	½	215	67
Basic meat mould, beef	½	330	70
Basic meat mould, chicken	½	165	70
Basic meat mould, lamb	½	330	70
Basic meat mould, pork	½	165	70
Basic meat mould, veal	½	165	70
Basic slimmers' cottage pie, beef	¾	405	69
Basic slimmers' cottage pie, chicken	¾	240	69
Basic slimmers' cottage pie, lamb	¾	405	69
Basic slimmers' cottage pie, pork	¾	240	69
Basic slimmers' cottage pie, veal	¾	240	69
Chicken curry	¾	345	61
Mexican chicken	¾	355	60

	CH Units	Calories	Page
Fish and Shellfish Dishes			
Baked herrings with vinegar sauce	¾	280	76
Fish cutlets in a foil parcel	½	160	77
Poached fish	¼	125	82
Shellfish cocktails, various	¾	60-65	89
Spicy mackerel (1)	½	130	85
Spicy mackerel (2)	¼	125	85
Sweet and sour baked fish	½	160	77
Egg Dishes			
Eggs on a bed of seafood	½	180	98
Salads			
Hot pepper salad	½	60	128
Salad Niçoise	½	90	125
Salad Dressings			
Yoghurt salad dressing	¼	20	132
Gravies and Sauces			
Pepper and tomato sauce	½	30	137
Slimmers' egg sauce	¾	75	136
Yoghurt and mint sauce	¼	20	137
Desserts			
Fruit jelly—Method 2	¾-1¼	25-30	152

Between 1 and 2 CH Units

	CH Units	Calories	Page
Meat, poultry and Offal Dishes			
Chicken and tomato casserole	1½	360	60
Liver parcels	1¾	275	62
Oxtail stew	1¾	425	64
Slimmers' savoury mince	1½	300	50
Stuffings			
Packeted	1½	35	72
Rice and liver	1	40	73
Fish and Shellfish Dishes			
Baked cod fillet	1½	105	87
Crabmeat stuffed tomatoes	1½	65	89
Fish casserole	1	145	81
Poached fish au gratin	1½	210	82
Shrimp stuffed tomatoes	1½	75	88
Smoked haddock in savoury sauce	1	145	86
Egg Dishes			
Tomato scramble	1	135	100

	CH Units	Calories	Page
Cheese Dishes			
Slimmers' cheese pie	1¾	320	104
Slimmers' quiche	1½	255	111
Spanish cheese	1½	465	108
Tomato and cheese casserole	1	185	108
Vegetable Dishes			
Vegetables with hard boiled egg	1¼	125	120
Vegetables with scrambled egg	1	275	119
Salads			
Coleslaw	1½	45	125
Gravies and Sauces			
Slimmers' savoury sauce	1¾	40	134
Desserts			
Basic egg custard	1¼	115	157
Fruit cream (depending on fruit)	1-2	110-130	149
Fruit fool (depending on fruit)	1½-2¼	50-65	148
Fruit mould (depending on fruit)	1¾-2¾	100-120	153
Fruit mousse (depending on fruit)	1-2	35-55	148
Fruit sorbet (depending on fruit)	1-2	35-55	149

Between 2 and 3 CH Units

	CH Units	Calories	Page
Meat, Poultry and Offal Dishes			
Basic meat casserole	2	400	48
Curried beef casserole	2	400	49
Kidneys in oxtail sauce	2¾	250	64
Lamb and kidney casserole	2	355	49
Lamb kebabs	2¾	390	53
Liver casserole	2¼	215	63
Slimmers' goulash, beef	2	400	49
Slimmers' goulash, veal	2	240	49
Sweet and sour pork	2	250	48
Stuffings			
Lemon	2	65	73
Mushroom, tomato and celery	2¼	60	72
Sausage and celery	2	205	74
Fish and Shellfish Dishes			
Baked stuffed fish	2½	340	79
Fish in cider	2½	170	81
Fruity baked fish	2½	160	77
Salads			
Jamaican savoury salad	2½	75	129

	CH Units	Calories	Page
Gravies and Sauces			
Slimmers' white sauce, coating	2½	70	134
Slimmers' white sauce, pouring	2	60	134
Desserts			
Baked fruit	2¼	50	150
Slimmers' custard	2½	70	157

Between 3 and 4 CH Units

	CH Units	Calories	Page
Fish and Shellfish Dishes			
Baked fish with egg sauce	3¼	250	76
Cheesey baked fish	3¼	325	76
Fish in wine	3½	190	81
Egg Dishes			
Soufflé, basic	3¼	255	96
Cheese Dishes			
Cauliflower cheese	3½	210	101
Cheese and banana salad	3	210	110
Cheese and cabbage casserole	3	260	109
Cheese puffs	3	280	111
Cheesey roes	3¼	360	108
Vegetable Dishes			
Tomato casserole	3	235	121
Vegetables with poached egg	3¾	225	119
Salads			
Orange and cauliflower salad	3¼	55	128
Oriental orange salad	3	60	127
Desserts			
Basic hot sweet soufflé	3¼	255	156
Fresh fruit salad	3¼	65	145

Between 4 and 5 CH Units

	CH Units	Calories	Page
Meat, Poultry and Offal Dishes			
Lamb stew	4	450	49
Polish slimmers' tripe	4	400	66
Sausage, grilled	4	400	52
Tripe and onions	4	335	65
Veal fricassée	4½	310	51
Stuffings			
Corn and onion	4¾	110	73

	CH Units	Calories	Page
Fish and Shellfish Dishes			
Fruity fillets	4	195	79
Vegetable Dishes			
Basic vegetable casserole	4	265	121
Vegetables au gratin	4	285	116
Salads			
Egg and potato salad	4¼	215	129

Between 5 and 6 CH Units

	CH Units	Calories	Page
Meat, Poultry and Offal Dishes			
Basic risotto, beef	5	265	68
Basic risotto, chicken	5	185	68
Basic risotto, lamb	5	265	68
Basic risotto, pork	5	185	68
Basic risotto, veal	5	185	68
Coq au vin	5½	425	61
Duck à l'orange	5	445	61
Pork with apple and cider	5	295	49
Vegetable Dishes			
Vegetables in wine	5	240	121
Desserts			
Fruit jelly—Method 1	5½	125	152

CH Units—6 and over

	CH Units	Calories	Page
Meat Dishes			
Bolognese	6	400	51
Stuffing			
Chestnut	7	195	74
Cheese Dishes			
Slimmers' macaroni cheese	6½	280	101

Index 1

Index 2

251

NUTRITION AND YOUR MIND

DR. GEORGE WATSON

Are you a fast oxidiser who burns his food up quickly? Or a slow one who burns it up slowly? Do you ever feel depressed, irritable or downright ill? If so, you may be suffering from the kind of brain starvation which is caused by the wrong diet. In this extraordinary new book Dr. George Watson draws on his many years of research to explain how your physical and mental health can be sensationally affected by the food you eat.

NUTRITION AND YOUR MIND explores a startling new theory about the relationship between nutrition and your health. The book also contains a questionnaire which will help you discover your own psycho-chemical type and a number of fascinating case histories.

CORONET BOOKS

SUPERNATURE
LYALL WATSON

Did you know that

A blunt razor blade left overnight inside a cardboard model of the Great Pyramid of Cheops will be sharp again in the morning?

A Chicago hotel porter can produce photographs by staring into cameras?

A potted plant registered emotion on a lie detector when an experimenter just decided to burn one of its leaves?

Lyall Watson has challenged scientific orthodoxy by applying new criteria to the investigation of supernatural phenomena. His fascinating and open-minded scientific study proves beyond doubt that science is stranger than the supernatural.

'A fascinating survey'   *Desmond Morris*

'A book of considerable importance, perhaps the most significant book about the "super-natural" to appear in the past decade ... very exciting'
Colin Wilson in *The Spectator*

CORONET BOOKS

ALSO AVAILABLE IN CORONET BOOKS

DR. GEORGE WATSON

☐ 19923 7   Nutrition and Your Mind   90p

LYALL WATSON

☐ 18833 2   Supernature   85p

ERNEST DUDLEY

☐ 19877 X   For Love of a Wild Thing   85p

HAZEL EVANS

☐ 20578 4   How to Cheat at Gardening   60p

PAUL WILKES

☐ 20014 6   Fitzgo   50p

STEPHEN BARLAY

☐ 19679 3   Sex Slavery   45p
☐ 19890 7   Aircrash Detective   95p

All these books are available at your local bookshop or newsagent, or can be ordered direct from the publisher. Just tick the titles you want and fill in the form below.
Prices and availability subject to change without notice.

CORONET BOOKS, P.O. Box 11, Falmouth, Cornwall.

Please send cheque or postal order, and allow the following for postage and packing:

U.K. – One book 18p plus 8p per copy for each additional book ordered, up to a maximum of 66p.

B.F.P.O. and EIRE – 18p for the first book plus 8p per copy for the next 6 books, thereafter 3p per book.

OTHER OVERSEAS CUSTOMERS – 20p for the first book and 10p per copy for each additional book.

Name...

Address...

....